THE POLITICAL THOUGHT OF JOHN MILTON

The Political Thought of John Milton

Charles R. Geisst

For my Mother and Father

© Charles R. Geisst 1984

All rights reserved. No part of this publication may be reproduced or transmitted, in any form or by any means, without permission

First published 1984 by
THE MACMILLAN PRESS LTD
London and Basingstoke
Companies and representatives
throughout the world

Printed in Hong Kong

British Library Cataloguing in Publication Data
Geisst, Charles R.
The political thought of John Milton.
1. Milton, John, *1608-1674*–Political science
2. Political science
I. Title
320.5′092′4   JC153.M/
ISBN 0-333-36602-6

Contents

	Acknowledgement	vi
	Preface	1
	Introduction	3
1	Logic and Human Affairs	5
2	Liberty and the Conscience	21
3	History and Society	39
4	Education	52
5	Liberty and the Commonwealth	71
6	Republican Thought and Historical Analysis	87
	Appendix I The Problem of *Essence*	106
	Appendix II Hartlib and Comenius	108
	Appendix III Filmer's Critique of Milton	110
	Bibliography	115
	Index	123

Acknowledgement

A special word of thanks to John B. Morrall of the London School of Economics and Political Science who supervised the original research in this essay.

Preface

Due to the lack of a complete works of Milton in a readily available form this study will cite two. The more popular and oft-quoted tracts will be cited in *John Milton: Complete Poems and Major Prose*, edited by Merritt Hughes. The longer and less popular works will be cited in the Columbia edition of Milton's complete works edited by Frank Patterson. Although the Columbia edition does contain all of Milton's works, it is not as readily available as Hughes text due to its age and if the reader should desire to check any of the references to the popular works he will find the shorter copy accessible.

The spelling of the quoted material contained in this essay has been modernized without any alteration to the originals. No other textual alterations have been made except in the last appendix where some of Filmer's quotations have been edited. In Filmer's reply to Milton it was usual for him to cite the page number of the Milton text to which he was referring. Those page numbers have been omitted in this essay.

The following abbreviations of Milton's works have been employed in the text to facilitate reference:

Apology—	An Apology for Smectymnuus
Commonwealth—	The Ready and Easy Way to Establish a Free Commonwealth
Hirelings—	Considerations Touching the Likliest Means to Remove Hirelings Out of the Church
PL—	Paradise Lost
PR—	Paradise Regained

The following journals have also been abbreviated in the text as well as in the bibliography:

HLQ—	Huntington Library Quarterly
HTR—	Harvard Theological Review
JBS—	Journal of British Studies
JEGP—	Journal of English and Germanic Philology
JHI—	Journal of the History of Ideas
JP—	Journal of Politics
JPh—	Journal of Philology

MLR — Modern Language Review
MP — Modern Philology
N + Q — Notes + Queries
PMLA — Publications of the Modern Language Association of America
PQ — Philological Quarterly
SEL — Studies in English Literature
SP — Studies in Philology
SR — Sewanee Review
UTQ — University of Toronto Quarterly

Introduction

The political thought of John Milton has never been considered as a systematic whole, originating in the state of nature and culminating in the free commonwealth. It has rather been analyzed through historical and literary techniques which by their very nature and method have failed to grasp the seminal ideas upon which Milton built his philosophic system. The approach used in this essay does not deny that Milton's poetry contains all of these ideas in some form or other, but seeks to accumulate this material *a posteriori* rather than rely upon the traditional methods of reading his prose as peripheral to his poetry or superimposing an historical occasion upon his thought in an attempt at elucidation. Even if Milton once stated that he wrote poetry with his right hand and prose with his left, it will not be considered specious here to view Milton as having been left-handed.

The traditional historical and literary methods of evaluating Milton's political thought have failed in two respects. The historical method has assumed that by tracing his ideas through the prose and its contemporary milieu one can come to a definitive conclusion concerning his political ideas. The literary approach has often denigrated the knowledge of mundane matters, or the "particulars" of political life, as being inapposite to the study of poetry in general, which rather tends to express the universal. Both methods have sought to topically dissect Milton's writings and assemble the results so as to critically evaluate his portent as a thinker. The result in a political context can often be (especially in the historical case) a logical hypallage.

For these reasons the approach employed herein has sought to isolate Milton's thought and substitute the ethical orientation so obvious in his work in place of historical contingencies. Although Milton's ethics have been scantly dealt with before, they have not been analyzed in a satisfactory political context. If viewed in this manner, it becomes obvious that ethics in general was the seminal framework around which Milton based his political and social thought. Regardless of the radicalism or heresy involved in some aspects of his political and religious ideas, this ethical orientation forms an almost neutral philosophic panorama within which Milton operated. He was able to borrow the basic ethical ideas of both Plato and Aristotle while usually avoiding the stricter doctrinal problems posed by their respective philosophic systems. In such a manner Milton's moral framework was bound to affront no one except perhaps Hobbes.

The method employed herein will thus seek to interpret Milton's political ideas through two perspectives; the theoretical and practical aspects of his thought. Chapter 1 strives to provide the conceptual framework of his overall "system." Chapter 2, concerning his evolution of the freedom of matter and his theology, is a significant part of the theoretical background of his political theory. Chapter 3, concerning society and history, provides the transitory phase between the "knowing why" and the "know how" of political endeavour and community. Chapter 4 concerning education illustrates the purely practical aspects of the means to attain the ideal commonwealth. The fifth chapter provides the final phase of the practical approach to politics in the embodiment of the commonwealth. Chapter 6 concludes.

Through this approach, which cannot claim to be inclusive, Milton's thought will be presented free of any extraneous issues which can tend to obfuscate the political philosophy of a man which has not been sufficiently treated to date. No one can claim to be in possession of all the intellectual material or tradition upon which Milton grounded his philosophy and the illustrative material contained in this essay has been chosen simply because it either elucidates Milton's thought to an extent where some academic borrowing or influence may be suspected or the relation is so obvious that it can not be overlooked. The end product will hopefully be Milton in as close to a true context as possible and not the Milton guilty of every political heresy in the book simply because he lived in a period of political heresy.

1 Logic and Human Affairs

The social philosophy of John Milton evolved out of a well-defined theology which contained numerous unorthodoxies. It employed ideas which appear to contradict each other without regard for philosophic consistency or coherence. This nebulous condition of Milton's social thought was not enhanced by the various mediums through which he chose to express it. Although Milton did write what may be considered a few serious political treatises, many of his prose writings were for the most part rhetorical as well as abrasive. But this compound problem does not obscure the fact Milton possessed a genuine social as well as religious philosophy. In this essay this philosophy will be viewed as a system, operating under the assumption that this framework was both logical and had a definite end in mind. While Milton was an ideologue and rhetorician par excellence, very little use was made of quixotic or philosophically unsound material in his works. When he described an idea with an upper-case letter it was always for a reason. While the roots of his thought were bound up in a quagmire of cross-currents, his explication was generally cogent and to the point. It does not require any serious reading between the lines to recognize that when Milton addressed himself to a correspondent such as Hartlib he also addressed himself to the larger, philosophic problem which Hartlib may, or may not, have symbolized. This was merely the style of this particular thinker. To use the hackneyed expression, Milton was a private man with a public cause. The private man never quite involved himself fully in the public realm but rather made his contribution by explicating contemporary ideas through a very private mode of thought. While the various endeavours he undertook required different types of expression, the current of his thought remained consistent and will be the focus of attention here.

This method of evaluating Milton is not new. Denis Saurat, in his *Milton: Man and Thinker*, treated this matter in a highly successful manner. This study is only an attempt to begin where Saurat terminated; with Milton's political ideas. As he originally stated:

It is finally, in applying his ideas to the affairs of men, that Milton tries to justify the ways of God. On that ground the question originally arose; here the whole philosophy of Milton reaches its ends.[1]

In order to achieve a valid understanding of Milton's political ideas, it is necessary to reconstruct his thought with an eye for social and ethical development. It becomes necessary to go one step beyond Saurat and attempt to show explicitly how Milton achieved this justification. With this *onus probandi* in mind, certain weaknesses in Milton's putative "system" will have to be made clear. Then the defects or weaknesses will not be so glaring in their original perspective.

I

The weakness of Milton's entire social philosophy was that he did not posit a concept of man's nature which remained constant throughout this thought. Without a valid conception of either the inherent goodness or inveterate evil of man on a social level, many of the institutional restraints and political devices in his theory appear inconsistent and somewhat paradoxical. Simply, his social philosophy was based upon a weak foundation.

The antithesis of such a position was found in many of Milton's contemporary writers, regardless of their philosophic persuasion. In his explicit attack on Hobbes, Ralph Cudworth found it necessary to drive to the heart of Hobbes' system in order to initiate his thesis:

> The foundation whereof is first laid in the villainizing of human nature; as that, which has not so much as any the least seeds, either of politicalness or ethicalness at all in it; nothing of equity or philanthropy . . . from all which it follows that nature absolutely dissociates and segregates men from one another, by reason of the inconsistency of those appetites of theirs that are carried out only to private good, and consequently that every man is, by nature, in a state of war and hostility against every man.[2]

Cudworth attempted to illustrate the inconsistencies which he felt arose from the Hobbesean state of nature. But to do so, he found it necessary to recognize that Hobbes' scheme was a logical delineation of the primal state and thus his attack centered upon that primal state.

Now Milton, like the Cambridge Platonists, took what amounted to an anti-Hobbesean position but this was not a stated fact as was Cudworth's. Man in his original state was one thing to Milton; man in the fallen state quite another. The two states had a common factor but this was not a matter of record. It rather takes a manner of close scrutiny to make it clear. While Hobbes "villainized" human nature in Cudworth's sense and the Cambridge group glorified it as a creation of God, Milton faltered. Rather than adopting either of the prevalent attitudes in their contemporary sense and following it through in a logical manner, he instead reverted to the original philosophies which embodied these ideas, viz. Augustinianism and, to an extent, Pelagianism. By doing so, he relied upon an historical tradition, which necessarily superimposed its own dictates, to act as a surrogate for an explicit statement concerning the nature of man which would have cleared up the duality for ever. It is, then, the synthesis of those two diametrically opposed positions that makes Milton's thought both original and difficult to come to grips with.

The common factor between these two diverse traditions in Milton's scheme is the fall of man from grace. Milton was a strict materialist in arguing that all matter was created *ex deo*. By this materialistic conception of creation, all things are seen as essentially good, having proceeded from God. But through the Fall mankind was placed in a state of sin. There is, then, a direct conflict between man and the state of created nature. Saurat solved this problem by calling it one of the duality of man.[3] But this distinction is a bit too facile. If there is such a state in man's composure it must be understood as one pertaining to his perceptive faculties rather than to a Jekyll and Hyde nature of the essence of his soul. Good, and especially its opposite, are not present in man through that Augustine metaphorically called the "seeds" of such. These two states of being are no more than a psychological matter of choice in Milton's thought. Now this is not to imply that evil and its ramifications are of little consequence but merely to illustrate that the initial act of choosing either good or evil was no more than exercising a rational choice. When the wrong choice was exercised through fallen reason, the appetitive soul gained hegemony over the rational bringing out the base in man's nature. In short, any religious considerations of moral action evident in Milton were initially based upon the incipient character of choice. It was from this rationalistic fountainhead that all distinctions involving choice between any options must be seen. The theological sense of good and evil and the ethical-political sense of just and unjust both have the same psychological foundation. And Milton was a subjective rationalist, i.e. this matter of reason and choice permeated all aspects of his thought. For him it symbolized the apogee of liberty, which could not be compromised in any sense at any time.

This nebulus state of affairs at the very outset of his theological and philosophical system is quite contrary to the ratiocination Milton displayed in his *Art of Logic*. While the second of these two books is more concerned with formal argumentation, the first advanced a theory of causation similar to that displayed in his delineation of social affairs. It is by applying this formal causative pattern specifically to Milton's political thought that enables his socio-philosophic "system" to become both limpid and orderly.

In his *Art of Logic* Milton defined causation in the four traditional categories; the efficient, material, formal, and final. Although he differed with Aristotle over their peculiar classification and accepted the position of Ramus, this does not appear to have affected the manner of explaining their simple relation to each other.[4] But regardless of the logic employed in his presentation, Milton conceived of the prime cause of all causes as God (the Absolute). From this position he proceeded to define all ensuing cause. Any deduction drawn from this method which does not posit God as the prime cause can only do so validly by positing something in his place as a genus of God the Absolute.

Milton's definition of the term cause gives a good introductory view of his philosophical language:

> A cause is that by force of which a thing exists . . . a cause is not badly defined as that which gives being to a thing . . . the cause, moreover, is not merely that by which the thing is, but also has been or will be.[5]

Cause does not have a merely functional role in Milton's logic. All causes contribute to the final as well as to the effect. Thus, God the efficient is only a part of God as final and cannot be fully understood as one cause of many. The same is true of political society. All causes of political life are an integral part of the end. Their contributory nature is more than simply functional in that they leave a definite impression upon the end which makes it distinctive.

The efficient cause was the cause of maintenance or procreation:

> For by the efficient is brought about the beginning of moving, yet the efficient is not within the effect.[6]

The efficient could work by itself under its own power or by accident through some extraneous force. But if this latter case were evident then the efficient would not be working under its own internal principle. The Son of God is a specific example here. He is the efficient cause of the Father working under the Father's power since both are two persons in the same God. The parents of an individual are also considered the efficient cause of that person's existence in that they are the procreative cause which brings about moving. But an important fact is evident here which will be examined later in a political context. Parents, as the efficient, are not totally within the effect.

The next cause in this sequence is matter, that cause from which a thing is what it is:

> . . . we know that matter is common to all entities and nonentities, not peculiar to sensible and corporeal things. But of whatever sort those things are, such the matter of them ought to be; the sensible should be composed of sensible things, the eternal of eternal things, and so in the rest.[7]

Matter's relation to the efficient is that of moved to mover:

> As the efficient cause is that which first moves, so the matter is that which is first moved; hence the efficient cause is called the principal cause of acting, matter the principal of being acted upon.[8]

The analogy initiated above can be continued here. As the parents are the efficient cause or movers of the life of the child, so the matter or life itself of that child is first moved. As Milton warned in the previous quote, matter cannot be used willy-nilly but must be kept in a strict proportion. Because the same causation is common to all levels of abstraction is not sufficient reason to destroy the causative scheme by interchanging genuses in regard to matter. Thus, the matter resultant or acted upon by the efficient cause or parents is the life of the child. The matter acted upon by the *Logos*, or creative agent of God, is all of life and created beings. But the *Logos* cannot directly be the efficient of life in an individual sense, although he is indirectly such, since this would interchange an eternal efficient for a corporeal one and vitiate the efficacy of such an explanatory technique.

Form constitutes the essence of a thing in this scheme:

> Form is the cause through which a thing is what it is . . . for the efficient produces the form not yet existing and induces it into the matter.[9]

This simply means that it is also a kind of effect of the efficient but in a specific sense rather than in the generic sense of matter. More importantly, in a theological sense, through form things take on their particular essence, or in human terms, personality or character:

> Form is produced in the thing simultaneously with the thing itself. Therefore the maxim is altogether true: when the form is given, the thing itself is given: when form is taken away, the thing is taken away.[10]

Continuing the human analogy, the life of matter finds its particular expression in the form, or personality, of the individual human being. As will be seen later, specifically on a theological plane, this form is called essence, through which the persons of the Trinity are differentiated.

The final cause, or end, is "... the cause for the sake of which a thing is."[11] But this end must imply a final good, not merely an ultimate or terminal point of causes. The teleological aspects of Milton's political society are evidenced here. Since all things were created good, they must have a final good as their end. If good was not the end of all created things, and especially political things, then they would exist for nothing, which is an impossibility.

The effect is "... that which comes from the causes."[12] Its relation to the causes proceeds in two directions, "... for the effect proves that the cause is or has been ... but the cause demonstrates why the effect should be."[13] In the analogy of procreation, life as matter makes clear the nature of man more so than does man the nature of life. Effect, as the expression of the causes, is "... as posterior (and) argues less weightily"[14] than the prior or anterior causes as such. In short, the composure of a thing is more important than the thing considered individually as a final product, although they are the same.

Social forces can be examined in this way in Milton's scheme but one important qualification is required. Man's fall must be either understood as an integral part of social causation or neglected in favor of man's original state of grace. But to take this later position would be unreal since the Fall was *fait accompli* in Milton's thought. Even by reducing causation to a mundane level of political affairs and its ethical orientation as a genus of God the Absolute, the Fall does not destroy the "sensible" proportion of this pattern by incorporating an abstract notion into corporal reality. The Fall was an ubiquitous force which had theological as well as political importance. Political causation as such is thus the same as cosmological causation in that the state of nature is common to both realms. God as the primal cause of all things is equally the primal cause of political affairs, but in order to keep this type of causation in a logical proportion, the scheme cannot conjecture him so. Also, the attempt to fit God into this pattern might tend to suggest a strong theocratic state of affairs in Milton, which is not the case. Thus, with all these factors taken into account, the following are postulated as the causes of political life:

efficient = a regenerative social process to rectify the sin of Adam
matter = the body politic
form = a republican type of government
end = the good political life of the Christian commonweath, where natural equality or liberty of conscience is preserved and protected.

The effect of these causes would be the ideal Christian political society which would lead to salvation. Education, as the efficient, first moves upon the body politic in the form of a republican government to produce the good political life in the nature of the Christian commonwealth. The intent of this essay is to illustrate how education could accomplish this feat. In a less logical sense, education will be considered the *sine qua non*, or simply, the necessary element in Milton's social thought. Now this is at odds with the spirit of Milton's statement in the *Art of Logic*:

> Hence it is understood that the cause *sine qua non*, as it is commonly called, is improperly and as though fortuitously considered a cause, as when the loss of something is called the cause of its finding, since the loss of necessity precedes finding. For, as Cicero teaches, cause ought not so to be understood that what precedes anything is considered its cause, but what efficiently precedes something; that is in such a way that the things exists by the power of it.[15]

It would appear quite logical to say that since the Fall, or loss of grace, preceded its reinstitution or finding in education much in the same way as the loss of necessity precedes finding, education cannot be considered the true efficient of society because the mover would in turn have an imperfect state as its primal cause in place of a genus of good. Yet in a less logical vein, Milton stated just the opposite in *Of Education* and it is with this in mind that education will be considered the prime factor in his thought. Logic serves as a vital tool which aids in keeping the various elements in Milton's scheme in their proper perspective, but if it is adhered to too strictly it can obviate some of the intricacies that make his thought original. It is easier to conceive of Milton's thought as a sequence of religious and social phenomena rather than as a narrow logical system simply because he was not as much a systematic philosopher as he was a coherent theorist.

II

Aside from the logic that comprises the framework of his thought, ethics was the dominant element in all of Milton's prose writings. It was the final mediator in all judgement, especially that of a political nature. The simple maxim that became a truism in his philosophy was initially quite an unfettered idea. It stated that if one was to be a good judge of an activity, one should have a knowledge of how that activity was best performed. But the traditions surrounding this idea in classical Greek thought suggest two interpretations possible. Did knowledge of the good of any activity suggest knowledge of an absolute norm or did it merely imply a relativistic conception based upon personal experience alone?

In a political sense, the relation of knowledge to the position considered must exist in two distinct ratios. It is evident on the level of individual competence, which would make a good cobbler a good judge of shoes, while at the same time existing on a quantified plane wherein the knowledge of one man is applied to political affairs. It was this political ratio Aristotle had in mind when he stated:

> The position thus being that we find men holding 1) that ruler and ruled should have different sorts of knowledge, and not one identical sort, and 2) that the citizen should have both sorts of knowledge and share in both.[16]

Political knowledge, or how to behave under different political relationships, was only a part of the idea of learning to judge by initially learning what the good was in a specific sense. However, the problem arises of exactly how much knowledge is required in the political context and of what kind.

A ruler rules many types of people, but does he necessarily need a knowledge of all their professions to rule them well? Since this is a natural impossibility except in the smallest of societies, the answer must be sought in a general concept of the good. And this good must be applicable to all situations. Henry More summed up this position well in his *Account of Virtue*. In Milton's case, the emphasis was upon knowing the good as well as being good in that one could not exist without the other. Knowledge must effectively precede action if both are to be aimed at a higher good. The state of goodness itself is known as grace and the faculty which aims to achieve it is reason.

The remaining question here is the specific nature of this good. Was it an absolute or merely relative? Obviously, it required both a knowledge of it and an outward display to render it valid. If it was used in an absolute sense, the form may never have been attained to perfection. But if Milton used it in a relative sense and accepted the absolute as understood, it then would become possible to use it as a paradigm of political conduct.

It was in this relativistic sense that Milton employed the idea. The Platonic theory of ideas was residual in his thought and found its expression in his poetic and eloquent prosaic language through which he expressed his adherence to the absolute form. But at the same time, he departed from what Aristotle described as the "whole of virtue" and immersed himself in a distributive application of these ideas in a political and even, to an extent, a theological manner. This is best evidenced in one of the major topics in Milton study – the relation of good and evil.

Two important presuppositions must be kept in mind when reading the account of good and evil in *Areopagitica*. First is Milton's conception of the nature of all created matter and the second is that good, then, is the intrinsic quality of all things. Evil was an extraneous element, introduced into nature and subsequently human affairs in point of time. Thus:

> Good and evil we know in the field of the world grew up together almost inseparably; and the knowledge of good is so involved and interwoven with the knowledge of evil, and in so many cunning resemblances hardly to be discerned, that those confused seeds of Psyche as an incessant labor to cull out and sort asunder, were not intermixed. It was from out the rine of one apple tasted, that the knowledge of good and evil, as two twins cleaving together, leaped forth into the world. And perhaps this is the doom which Adam fell into of knowing good and evil, that is to say, of knowing good by evil. As therefore the state of man now is, what wisdom can there be to choose, what continence to forbear without the knowledge of evil.[17]

Now if the relation of these two forces is unorthodoxically stated, Milton's source for it was not. In the *Ethics* Aristotle stated:

> Now, we often gain knowledge of a) a characteristic by the opposite characteristic, and b) of characteristics of those things in which they are exhibited.[18]

Milton's description of the two forces was no more than a paraphrase of this quote. At the basis of this seemingly backward method of knowing good was that intermediate agent between God and man which was truly in a fallen state. In a sense, the Fall story was nothing more than a symbolic presentation of perverted reason divorcing itself from its real potential through pride. Thus, the problem of good and evil must be viewed through the eyes of a rationalist. Naturally, evil could not be introduced coextensively into the world as an equal force with good due to the nature of the act or decree of creation, which will be dealt with in a subsequent chapter. But the creation of the world is not at issue here; what is is simply the perspective of human affairs. The sin of Adam illustrates that reason was not perfect and introduced mankind to evil coextensively with good. In short, evil cannot exist except as a choice of intrinsic good, which immediately implies a perceptive faculty which can distinguish between the two. Irrational beings were not subject to this distinction; only angels and men were capable.

The second presupposition considered here concerning these forces must also take into account that Milton considered a fall from reason tantamount to a fall from grace. This was the result of equating knowledge of the good (reason) with the state of being good (grace). Knowing a quality through its opposite characteristic required superior intellect in this case since knowing a quality exhibited in other things of like degree would obviously be the prime, as well as easier, way of attaining knowledge of the good. There is always the imminent danger of never knowing a true degree of good but rather being content with its opposite. Only corrective measures can reinforce the intellect against perverted extraneous forces. Whether such measures can indeed be applied is an answer this discussion will have to seek in Milton's concept of the state of nature and finally in his educational theory. But first, good and evil should be briefly examined to elucidate their political nature.

The political equivalent of these two terms is just and unjust. Aristotle, in the *Ethics*, described the different kinds of justice, especially the two which are different in degree from the whole. The first type, distributive, is justice in a proportional sense.[19] A person is given his due in payment of just action. The payment is proportionate to his contribution. The unjust in this case is that which would violate the proportion and grant him an inexact due. The relation of this to evil is as follows:

> The reverse is true in the case of evil: for in relation to a greater evil the lesser evil counts as a good, since the lesser evil is more desirable than the greater and since what is desirable is good and what is more desirable is a greater good.[20]

Although the inverse ratio here is based upon the semantical difference between the two terms, the relation of just to unjust is the same as that of good and evil.

The second partial form is justice of rectification. This is justice as a median in a juristic or legal sense. In this case, two persons appear before the law to rectify a wrongdoing. "As the unjust in this case is inequality, the judge tries to restore the equilibrium."[21] The judge attempts to restore equilibrium in a mediatorial sense, i.e. by giving back to the injured party what was deprived him. If two persons have equal shares in something and one deprives the other of part of his share, the mediator seeks to restore the balance in an arithmetical fashion. This is distinctly different from the distributive case where the just was based upon a geometric sense of what was due.

These two conceptions of the just led Aristotle to a discussion of justice in political bodies in the *Politics*, although emphasis there was on the distributive. It is in respect to just and equal that Milton elucidated this premise of distributive justice when he proposed his commonwealth. The equal, in this case, will be equated with the superior implying a general inequality. But as will be shown, this inequality was only valid politically. Justice as rectification could still be adhered to in the instance of a violation of natural right but not in the sense of granted political privileges. But in order to avoid overemphasizing this point in relation to Aristotle or any inconsistencies which may arise in Milton's particular case, this discussion will now turn to the last important factor in Milton's thought before considering his theology.

III

The state of nature in Milton's thought can be misunderstood just as easily as the true relation of good and evil. Nature was a term used freely in his vocabulary but was not a surrogate for the authority of Scripture. The written word of God, as expressed in the Gospels in particular, was the ultimate source of authority to Milton. No recourse to any other authority was necessary. The state of nature was only an expression of God's goodness and benevolence; and free of evil. The problem of evil was not indicative of a natural state, since,

> Evil into the mind of God or Man
> May come and go, so unapprov'd, and leave
> No spot or blame behind.[22]

A difference is evidenced between the natural state and the psychological, cognitive process of reason. Milton did not believe that one could sin by merely entertaining a sinful notion. Adam's sin also included action. Thus, there was a difference in thinking about evil and performing it in accordance with perverted reason. As was shown earlier, knowing evil as well as good was an essential part of the cognitive process. The performance of evil was in accord neither with reason nor the state of nature.

Milton was a rationalist in the true sense of the word. By elevating reason to the fullest he accordingly defined good as right reason in accord with nature. But this concordance did not suggest that nature was a power in itself:

> There are some who pretend that nature or fate is this supreme power: but the very nature of nature implies that it must owe its birth to some prior agent, or, to speak properly, signifies in itself nothing; but means either the essence of a thing or that general law which is the origin of everything, and under which everything acts; on the other hand, fate can be nothing but a divine decree emanating from some almighty power.[23]

Nature was the universal, cosmic order to Milton. It signified the whole to which any part belonged, but not an origin. Nature was not a cause of association but merely the ambiance within which causation occurred. It was for this reason that art could find its perfect paradigm in nature:

> There are in a picture two things – the subject or archtype and the art of painting – so in the discovery of an art, nature or practice and the example of skilful man correspond to the archtype, and logic to

the art of the painter – natural logic at least, which is the very faculty of reason in the mind of man, according to that common saying: Art imitates nature.[24]

The question may be raised here of whether nature was not the true divinity of mankind due to its direct accessibility through such expressive forms as art. And Milton was guilty of a sort of pantheism. The natural order was so permeated with goodness as a result of creation that only a fine line distinguished the divinity from his creation. Although Milton did not posit a strong conception of human nature upon which to build his social thought, it is obvious that this was not necessary in his mind due to the conception of universal goodness. The true foundation of Milton's social philosophy is not to be found in any particular statement concerning the nature of man but rather in his theology. The difficulties that sin provides in his thought are illustrative of this.

IV

The problem of sin in Milton's scheme is indicative of all the various dichotomies and tensions which characterize his thought. In searching for the prime example of ambivalence in his system, sin is found to embody all the obvious problems in one, symbolic form. This particular problem evolves out of the concept Milton employed when viewed in contradistinction to his general sanguine outlook for human destiny.

The idea of original sin as employed by St. Augustine in the *City of God* is perhaps the most pessimistic theory of all-encompassing guilt propounded anywhere. It was based upon the theory of generation which literally understood Adam as the father of the entire human race:

> The fact is that the human race took its rise from one man whom God created first, as we are assured in Holy Scripture, which has, and rightly so, marvellous authority throughout the world and among all nations.[25]

Man's disobedience, as much a fall from grace as from reason, became an inherent part of that same generative process:

> Therefore the entire human race contained in the first man when

that conjugal couple received the divine sentence condemming them to punishment, and man reproduced what man became, not when he was being created, but when he was sinning and being punished, at least as far as the origin of sin and death is concerned.[26]

The result of this act was that man perpetrated upon himself an inherent essence of degradation, guilt, and sin as well as death. This happy combination is what N.P. Williams has called the theory of "seminal identity" (in *The Ideas of the Fall and of Original Sin*). Thus,

> God created man upright, for He is the author of natural beings, not surely, of their defects. Man, however, when he was willingly corrupted and justly condemned, engendered corrupt and condemmed offspring. For we were all in that one man who fell into sin through the woman who was made from him before sin. We did not yet have individually created and apportioned shapes in which to live as individuals, what already existed was the seminal substance from which we were to be generated. Obviously, when this substance was debased through sin and shackled with the bond of death in just condemnation, no man could be born of man in any other condition.[27]

Milton employed a similar use of sin in his chapter concerning the Fall in the *Christian Doctrine*. This was similar to the Augustinian theory of generation:

> The sin which is common to all men is that which our first parents, and in them all their posterity, committed, when, casting off their obedience to God, they tasted the fruit of the forbidden tree.[28]

But instead of total degradation, the first parents rather passed on to posterity the innate ability to sin, termed evil concupiscence. As will be shown later, Milton adhered to this theory in a partial sense. With what has already been said regarding the relation of good and evil in Milton's thought, it is obvious that this theory could not have been borrowed in its entirety by him. But the theory of generation was used. The point to be kept in mind concerning Milton's use of this idea is that man's propensity to sin can never be removed although he may himself be regenerate. He will still pass on this condition to his posterity. Thus, it was not the theory of seminal identity which is of prime importance here but the conclusion which Augustine reached: "As a result, what came initially as punishment to the first human beings who sinned also follows as a natural consequence in the rest who are born."[29] Milton's own version of the idea stated:

> For Adam being the common parent and head of all, it follows that, as in the covenant, that is, in receiving the commandment of God, so also in the defection from God, he either stood or fell for the whole human race.[30]

What Milton did not accept was the Augustinian idea of the total destructiveness of sin upon mankind. Neither Milton nor Augustine accepted that evil had a divine origin but Milton did not go the extreme opposite in imputing sin's full consequence to future generations.

The psychological nature of good and evil does not vitiate the intrinsic goodness of the natural order. In short, man could not create his own reality, or natural state, by choosing evil over good since the nature of his perceptive powers was limited. While the variables of Milton's thought may have at times tended towards the pessimistic, the primal and final causes always reverted back to the state of goodness. Thus, the real key to understanding Milton's system should initially be sought in his theology. This was no doubt what prompted him to state that: ". . . certainly theology will better discuss providence than will logic."

NOTES

1. Denis Saurat, *Milton: Man and Thinker* (London, 1946), p. 152.
2. "The True Intellectual System of the Universe" cited in *The Cambridge Platonists*, ed. G. Cragg (New York, 1968), pp. 354 f.
3. Saurat, *op. cit.*, p. 124.
4. Aristotle, according to Milton, divided the four causes into genera and named them internal and external; internal being the efficient and matter, external being form and end. Ramus declined this to avoid semantical problems arising from this position; see *The Works of John Milton*, ed. F. Patterson, et al. (New York, 1936), XI, p. 55. – hereafter cited as *Works*.
5. *Works* XI, pp. 29 f.
6. *Ibid.*, p. 33.
7. *Ibid.*, p. 53.
8. *Ibid.*, p. 51.
9. *Ibid.*, p. 59.
10. *Ibid.*, p. 61.
11. *Ibid.*, p. 63.
12. *Ibid.*, p. 71.

13. *Ibid.*
14. *Ibid.*
15. *Ibid.*, p. 31.
16. Aristotle, *Politics*, trans. Ernest Baker (New York, 1962), 1277a 11.
17. John Milton: *Complete Poems and Major Prose*, ed. Merritt Hughes (New York, 1957), p. 728 – hereafter cited as *Hughes*; Milton's anti-Augustinianism is evident in this particular passage. Augustine traced the introduction of evil to those creatures who possessed a will (*Confessions*, VII). He and Milton would generally be agreed on this point. However, Augustine also posited that there was only one unchangeable good and that was God. All other things were subject to change because they were created *ex nihilo* (*City of God*, XII). This is in direct opposition to Milton's creation *ex deo*. While sharing the same distaste for the perversions of the will, the two are otherwise diametrically opposed over the character of good in nature.
18. 1129a 17–19.
19. *Nichomachean Ethics* trans. M. Oswald (New York, 1962), 1131b 16; also *Politics* 1280b 1.
20. *Ethics*, 1131b 20.
21. *Ibid.*, 1132a 7.
22. *PL* V, 117–119; C.S. Lewis pointed out that the idea of latent evil in God was a heretical one but can not be attributed to Milton. Concerning this quote from *PL* he stated: "Since the whole point of Adam's remark is that the approval of the will alone makes a mind evil and that the presence of evil as an object of thought does not since our common sense tells us that we no more become bad by thinking of badness than we become triangular by thinking about triangles."; see a *Preface to Paradise Lost* (Oxford, 1967), p. 84. Also see C.R. Geisst, "Milton and Ambrose on Evil", *N + Q*, vol. 23, no. 5–6, p. 233.
23. *Works*, XIV, p. 27.
24. *Ibid.*, XI, p. 11.
25. *City of God*, trans. P. Levine (London, 1966), XII, 9.
26. *Ibid.*, XIII, 3.
27. *Ibid.*, 4.
28. *Works* XV, p. 193.
29. *City of God*, XIII, 3.
30. *Works*, XV, p. 183.

2 Liberty and the Conscience

The term liberty carries a dual connotation. In the course of making an historical judgement the primary nature of liberty is often neglected in favour of its secondary quality, the relation of the individual and the state. The problem of conscience and its relation to man in political society is as old as that society itself, but this is not sufficient reason to overlook it in favour of historical judgements designed to place it in its "proper perspective". The danger of treating the concept of liberty of an individual thinker in its quantitative sense only is that the material can sometimes present itself as second-hand knowledge with its primary qualities being explained away merely as understood or implied. No such assumption will be made here concerning this concept as employed by Milton. It appears that this very fallacy has led more than one Milton scholar to draw a spurious conclusion in appraising his works. Milton granted all Christians freedom of religion and tolerated all sects except one – Roman Catholicism. This fact can lead the student of Milton to more than one conclusion concerning his views on toleration. One may draw the somewhat sophisticated historical conclusion that Milton's tolerationist views had one flaw, or that the objectiveness in Milton's "lofty" libertarian thought "revealed a narrowness" in his denial of toleration to Roman Catholicism. It will be the intent of this chapter to illustrate that there is neither flaw nor narrowness in Milton's thought unless it be on the part of the historian who would make such a judgement.

Milton's conception of the efficient means of political society is at first confusing when compared to his concept of its origins and ends. In keeping with the dominant motif of his period, Milton relied heavily upon the revival of classical antiquity to provide the practical paradigm upon which to build a conception of politics. Thus, he was able to speak of a commonwealth and its government in ostensibly modern terms while at the same time drawing logical conclusions concerning society itself which tend to confuse the reader who is caught unaware of the undercurrent of his thought. Milton's language allies him with the early theorists of modern pluralistic societies; his philosophy with those of antiquity. The origins of conscience are rooted in theology; the origins of political obligation in antiquity. Only his language appears *prima facie* modern.

Liberty in political society had a definitely negative connotation to Milton:

> It is work good and prudent to be able to guide one man; of larger extended virtue to order well one house; but to govern a Nation piously and justly, which only is to say happily, is for a spirit of the greatest size and divinest mettle . . . yet there is no art that hath been more cankered in her principles, more soiled and slubbered with aphorisming pedantry than the art of policy . . . this is the masterpiece of the modern politician, how to qualify and mould the sufferance and subjection to the length of that foot that is to tread on their necks, how rapine may serve itself with the fair, and honourable pretences of public good, how the puny law may be brought under the wardship and control of lust and will . . .[1]

Regardless of his use of the rhetorical, political necessity dictated that the neck must be tailored to the foot to avoid undue pressure and it is with this neck that the discussion of Milton's concept of liberty must begin.

The problem with which Milton wrestled was that of obedience. The Petrine doctrine from the *Acts of the Apostles* (5:29) provides the most lucid example of this. As St. Peter stated to the Sanhedrin: "We must obey God rather than man." Milton was in full accord with this maxim. To obey God was to obey one's conscience. The primary form of all liberty was religious, i.e. Christian liberty. The Petrine doctrine was included in his personal definition:

> Christian liberty is that whereby we are loosed as it were by enfranchisement, through Christ our deliverer, from the bondage of sin and consequently from the rule of law and man; to the intent that being made sons instead of servants, and perfect men instead of children we may serve God in love through the Guidance of the spirit of Truth.[2]

Christian liberty was both fundamental and intrinsic to political liberty and society. It could not and did not change its nature due to the rule of man and human laws. Ideally, the best form of civil society was that of the Christian commonwealth; an idea woven with Aristotelian elements into Milton's *Commonwealth*. Whether or not society could be specifically tailored to the requirements of this commonwealth will be taken up in a subsequent chapter but this concept of obedience to God alone is the harbinger of the problem Milton eventually faced in his outline for the body politic.

A further clue to his idea of conscience can be found in his autobiographical passage in the *Second Defense*. He went on to perceive three species of liberty essential to life – religious, domestic, and civil. Concerning the second he stated:

> As this seemed to involve three material questions, the conditions of the conjugal tie, the education of the children, and the free publication of thoughts, I made them objects of distinct consideration.[3]

It must be noted that these three forms of domestic liberty were quite distinct from the civil. This adds a twofold character to the concept of liberty and its relation to the individual. The first will concern itself with liberty in a theological and religious sense through the state of nature. The second will concern itself with the preserving of this inherent liberty in social relationships. The reason why these forms may be divorced from the purely civil is that they depend upon one faculty which is equally intrinsic to the state of nature – reason. Without right reason man cannot function according to his full potential. This is not to imply that reason as such was lacking in society but only to emphasize that this faculty is a human element which must be nurtured individually before it could be nurtured collectively.

The source material from which to draw for an explication of Milton's ideas concerning inward liberty will be arbitrary in this case due to the scope of this essay. Liberty in its Christian context certainly finds its best expression in his *Christian Doctrine*. The liberty of domestic relationships is best found in *Areopagitica, Of Education*, and parts of the *Doctrine and Discipline of Divorce*. To draw political conclusions from this concept of Christian liberty, which necessarily involves examining some of his theological doctrines, is an even more arbitrary matter. For this reason the *Christian Doctrine* will first be examined for its practical merits and the peculiarities of his theological thought. The unorthodoxy of these religious ideas gives perhaps the best illustration of what Milton meant by inward liberty; the free expression of an idea in accordance with reason, no matter how heretical.

In order to delineate the concept of liberty according to conscience, it will be necessary to begin where Milton did, at the beginning of what he considered Christian doctrine. To grasp this fully an understanding must be reached of what Milton conceived of as perception. Human faculties perceived Christian doctrine by divine revelation; disclosed to mankind through the Scriptures. Doctrine was not disclosed to man by any other means, e.g. philosophical interpretation or human laws. Specifically, it was to be perceived by each individual as his own interpreter of Scripture. It was to be comprehended through two inseparable divisions, faith (the knowledge of God) and love (the worship of God). It must be noted that faith in this sense ". . . does not mean the habit of believing, but the things to be habitually believed."[4]

I

Milton divided the efficiency of God into two parts, the internal and the external. The internal efficiency was free of all extraneous agents. His decrees were of this nature. These decrees were sub-divided into two divisions, the general and the special:

> God's general decree is that whereby He has decreed from all eternity of His most free and wise and holy purpose, whatever He willed, or whatever He was Himself about to do.[5]

But this general decree was not to be understood as absolute to the control of all things. Those actions which were left to the power of free agents were not included in the absolute sense of the decree. While God has not decreed all things absolutely, obviously all things do fall within his all-encompassing scope due to his omniscience. Here the wisdom of God was relied upon to explain this difficulty. God's wisdom and foreknowledge were considered the same. Thus, he was able to know of man's fall by his wisdom without interfering with the free agency, or will, of man. Man's fall was not specifically a decree or included in a decree of God. If it had been, as normal human reason might assume, then it would have been in contradiction of the general decree. But since man was a free agent, no problem arises in viewing his self-destruction as a matter of his own volition. In short, since man had the power of choice which was determined from all eternity as a part of a general decree, the action which caused his fall could not have specifically been a part of this same decree without proving self-contradictory:

That the will of God is the first cause of all things is not intended to be denied, but we do not separate his prescience and wisdom from His will, much less do we think them subsequent to the latter in point of time. Finally, the will of God is not less the universal first cause, because he has himself decreed that some things should be left to our own free will, than if each particular event had been decreed necessarily.[6]

This concept comes into conflict with some of the more popular doctrines of Milton's day, notably Calvinism. Milton considered predestination as a special decree of God. While foreknowledge of the Fall was acknowledged, it did not imply predestination. This fact was limpidly stated in *Paradise Lost*:

Foreknowledge had no influence on their fault,
Which had no less prov'd certain unforeknown.
So without least impulse or shadow of Fate.
Or aught by me immutably foreseen,
They tresspass, Authors to themselves in all
Both what they judge and what they choose; for so
I form'd them free, and free they must remain,
Till they enthrall themselves; I else must change
Thir nature, and revoke the High Decree
Unchangeable, Eternal, which ordain'd
Thir, freedom: they themselves ordain'd thir fall[7]

Predestination was reserved for mankind out of the pity of God. It was a special decree before the foundation of the world. It was not the same as election in the Calvinist sense. Election in Milton's lexicon was not to be considered a term for a chosen people, but was rather synonomous with eternal predestination or considered as special election, i.e. the election of all to salvation. Reprobation, equally, was not a part of predestination or of a decree. As no special group had the key to salvation by virtue of a decree, neither did any have the odious key to damnation. God's special decree stated that all can be considered specially elect if they maintain faith.

The problem of evil arises here in considering man's destiny. If the Fall had been included in an absolute decree of God, then sin might logically have been imputed to him as well. Evil as a choice of mankind would have then found a scapegoat in God and vindicate itself merely as of divine ordination. But as has already been shown, evil remained through choice, the discretionary agent of man. It was not a part of any decree of God, either general or special, and cannot be imputed to him.

The act of creation was classified by Milton as a species of God's eternal efficiency. This particular argument clearly has more cogent and practical ramifications than some of Milton's other theological discourses. By this act, God created by his will and is the sole cause of all things, which he embraces within himself; the efficient, material, formal and final. It may be said that the Father is he *of whom, from whom, through whom*, and *on account of whom* all things exist. It will be shown later that the Son is only he *by whom* all things exist, an efficient cause only.

The act of creation amplifies one of Milton's more unorthodox beliefs. Having acknowledged God as the cause of all causes, the problem of material formation arises:

> Therefore the material cause (of Creation) must be either God, or nothing (since nothing else existed except God). Now nothing is not a cause at all, and yet it is contended that forms, and above all, human forms, were created out of nothing.[8]

Milton rejected the concept of creation *ex nihilo* in favor of creation *ex deo* since creation must have logically proceeded from God, nothing being the only alternative. It would not be consistent to argue that God could be the cause of all things except matter[9]:

> Since therefore it has (as I conceive) been satisfactorily proved under the guidance of Scripture, that God did not produce everything out of nothing, but of Himself, I proceed to consider the necessary consequence of this doctrine, namely, that if all things are not only from God, but of God, no created thing can be finally annihilated.[10]

Having established the true nature of Creation, Milton then introduced mankind, infused with a measure of divine influence. Man did not exist separately from his soul; the whole man was considered in expressed terms a living soul. The soul did not exist apart from the body and was propagated from father to son. God did not busy himself with creating a new soul for every act of human reproduction. This was logical to Milton since if God were to create a new soul for every product of the human sexual act, then the new soul would necessarily have to be pure, having proceeded from God. This would have created the paradox of explaining how man was still born in a state of sin. A pure soul could not be fused with an unchaste body. To admit otherwise would be to subscribe to the doctrine of the separation of form and matter, which Milton rejected. The rational soul must be communicated by generation in the same manner as sin; from the soul, as well as the loins of Adam, tainted by original sin. The conclusive argument was as follows:

> Lastly, on what principle of justice can sin be imputed through Adam to that soul, which was never either in Adam, or derived from Adam? In confirmation of which Aristotle's argument may be added, the truth of which in my opinion is indisputable. If the soul be equally diffused throughout any given whole, and throughout every part of that whole, how can the human good, the noblest and most intimate part of all the body, be imagined destitute and devoid of the soul of the parents, or at least of the father, when communicated to the son by the laws of generation? It is acknowledged by the common consent of almost all philosophers, that every form, to which class the human soul must be considered as belonging, is produced by the power of matter.[11]

This same principle will naturally hold true regarding death. Milton flatly rejected the Catholic doctrine that the soul and the body separate at death with the former arising or descending, as the case may be.

> The common definition (of the death of the body) which supposes it to consist in the separation of soul and body, is inadmissable.[12]

When the body died, the whole man, both body and soul, perished as well with the spirit waiting for its eventual redemption by Christ.[13] With the espousal of this doctrine Milton expressed what is known as the mortalist heresy, i.e. that the soul is somehow mortal like the body. Death is the natural concomitant of sin. This is death in the first degree. Spiritual death is the loss of divine grace. This is the second degree of death. The third degree is that of the body itself.[14] Although distinguished by degrees, death could not separate form and matter. It rather adhered to the law of nature which was immanent in Creation.

Man's relation to this doctrine was quite simple, Adam was commanded not to eat of the forbidden fruit as an act of obedience. No works whatever were required of him; ". . . a particular act only was forbidden."[15] Adam could have been saved by faith alone; by obeying God's commandment. Faith was given precedence above works of law, even the Mosaic law. Good works were the manifestation of faith.

The Catholic doctrine that a superabundance of good works may purchase eternal life was an impossibility. Good works were merely a part of the worship of God: faith was part of the knowledge of him:

> Good works are those which we perform by the spirit of God working in us through true faith, to the glory of God the assured hope of our salvation and the edification of our neighbor.[16]

To be saved, a man need only to have faith since the knowledge of God should dictate prudence to the will, from which all works spring.

The final aspect of inward liberty considered here will be that of God's governance of man. The truth of God was manifest to man through Scripture:

> Inasmuch however, as it was not possible for our liberty either to be perfect or made fully manifest till the coming of Christ our deliverer, liberty must be considered as belonging in an especial manner to the Gospel, and as consorting therewith.[17]

It is at this juncture that the conception of real liberty becomes apparent. Man was enthralled until Christ set him free, concomitantly giving him back his original liberty as well. And the words and deeds of Christ are manifest through the Gospels. Since Christ and his word have been equated with true liberty, it is necessary to turn this discussion to Milton's greatest unorthodoxy, his subordinationism. But before doing so, it is appropriate here to briefly reconstruct these previous arguments in a manner from which we can discover the consequences of man's actions, especially in the way they affect his political behaviour.

Thus far it has been established that man was created a free agent and that foreknowledge had nothing to do with his fall. This was rather a matter of his own free will. The act of creation itself proceeded *ex deo* rather than *ex nihilo* although man received only as much of the divine virtue as was his ability to receive. After the Fall, Christ appeared to free man's soul from the slavery of damnation and by doing so became the true source of his liberty. Man's being was considered inseparable regarding form and matter; the whole man being the soul. At death man died fully and waited for his redemption by Christ. The Gospels are the word of Christ and the prime source of liberty to mankind. Man's cause in all things is God, his end is God and his matter was derived from God. It would appear that no immediate consequences can be drawn from these facts. However, an earthly realm does exist which appears far-removed indeed from such causation. It is possible to separate this extraterrestrial realm from the terrestrial, which was created by man's reason. This second realm finds its immediate causation in human reason much in the same way that the governance of the universe finds its total causation in God. By his proliferation and actions as a free agent, man found himself in need of a civil society. The agency by which man functions in this society and at the same time worships God is reason. When reason becomes perverted through extraneous forces, it must be rectified by human means, viz. education. Thus, education did not have to be primarily religious in Milton's sense although it certainly had to be moral or ethical. A great deal of his educational theory was based upon pagan authors. Rectitude in a social sense depended upon setting reason aright; in matters of salvation it depended upon faith and love.

II

If the greatest test of a theory of liberty is its practical application then Milton's theology concerning the nature of Christ is the best example apt to be found in his thought. His ideas on this subject are generally deemed his most heretical. It is dubious whether any political contingency can be drawn from his subordinationism since ethical-political theory would be less concerned over the relationship of the Son to the Father than in the very fact that the Son does somehow exist. This portion of his thought is merely illustrative for present purposes; the examination of Milton's subordinationism as his greatest unorthodoxy and at the same time an example of his own conception of true liberty.

The Son of God was classified as a result of generation, a part of God's external efficiency. He was not to be considered a part of internal efficiency:

> This point appears certain, notwithstanding the arguments of some of the moderns to the contrary, that the Son existed in the beginning, under the name of logos or word, and was the *first* of the whole creation, by whom *afterwards* all other things were in both heaven and earth.[18]

The Son was also not to be considered co-essential with the Father. If he was, Milton pointed out that there would be no reason for calling him son. This was not a weakness in Milton's logic although it would appear so at first. He was only appealing to human reason in cases like this; the type of reason which made nomenclature necessary in the first place. The generation of the Son proceeded from a decree and of the Father's own will.[19] But they do not possess the same will. Thus, ". . . it is manifest that these who do not have the same will cannot have the same essence."[20] Confusion arose concerning the Trinity through those who mistook the nature of the Son for that of the Father. A good deal of the *Christian Doctrine* (Book I, chapter 5) is devoted to setting this supposed logical inconsistency aright. Milton deplored the fact that those who held to the doctrine of the unity of God nevertheless maintained that the Father alone was not God. Furthermore, the Son does not partake of the divine substance of the Father if *substance* is equated with *essence* in this case in the context of the *Christian Doctrine*. If the two terms are considered the same, then Milton would have espoused an essentially Arian doctrine, denying any common entity to the Trinity. But if a distinction is made between them considering *substance* as the substratum of the Godhead and *essence* as that peculiar to the distinct person in terms of the Trinity, then the position would still be basically trinitarian but at the same time subordinationist.[21] But, as Milton originally tried to show; "he who is not co-essential with God the Father, cannot be co-equal with the Father."[22] To divide the same essence numerically would have been tantamount to reducing it, which simply was not possible. The Son is the *logos*, the word of God, not co-equal with him in terms of essence. This being the case, this study must next turn its attention to the place of the Son in Milton's theology.

The Father is the cause of all causes, as shown above. In distinction to this, the ". . . Son is not he *of whom* but only *by whom* . . ." all things exist:

> It is evident therefore that when it is said all things were by him, it must be understood as a secondary or delegated power; and that when the particle by is used in reference to the Father, it denotes the primary cause . . .[23]

Christ's role is that of mediator between God and man, although not being wholly human. By the same standard, he cannot be considered as of the same nature or person as God the Father without providing the dubious distinction of being a mediator unto himself. The mediatorial function of the Son is distinguished from that of his capacity of Creator, whereby he is called the "first born of every creature." The Son's role is that of an efficient cause, it is him *by whom* all things exist.

This nature of the Son is mutable. Since Milton proved that the Son proceeded from the Father and is now separate from him, a certain change occurred making him mutable in distinction to the immutable Father. Being immutable, the Father cannot create as such. He therefore retained his immutability by designating the power of creator to the Son. The Son is thus lower in dignity than his Father although still of the same substance.

Relatively little is said of the role of the Holy Spirit in Milton's cosmology. The basis for this neglect of the putative third person was attributed to lack of evidence for it found in Scripture. By attempting to derive its function from Scriptural passages, Milton was led to the conclusion that the Spirit was inferior to both Father and Son. It was declared subservient in all things:

> Lest however we should not be altogether ignorant who or what the Holy Spirit is, although Scripture nowhere teaches us in express terms, it may be collected from the passages quoted above that the Holy Spirit, inasmuch as he is a minister of God, and therefore not a creature, was created or produced of the substance of God, not by a natural necessity, but by the free will of the agent, probably before the foundations of the world were laid, but later than the Son, and far inferior to him.[24]

It is interesting to note that the *Christian Doctrine* was not discovered and translated into English by Bishop Sumner until 1823. This seems to have let Milton off the hook as far as political or doctrinal reverberations went in his own lifetime. But as he would have undoubtedly foreseen, it could have proved detrimental to his immortality as a poet. The book's discovery has sent more than one Milton scholar back to re-reading *Paradise Lost* seeking undiscovered aberrations in his supposedly orthodox thought. In light of these charges of heresy which followed the publication, Milton retained one academic trump card in his deck. He rooted his theological thought in the period of ante-Nicean Christianity, closely allying himself with the early Church controversialists. This type of "pre-dogmatic" allegiance was not necessarily espousing heresy to Milton since the concept of the trinity was not affirmed in retaliation to Arius until the Council of Nicea, called by Constantine in 325. He was merely playing one-upmanship with his future critics by declaring himself a non-dogmatic, primitive Christian.

The historical argument employed in this method illustrates his atavism, or what some have called his recidivism. In the *Christian Doctrine* he stated:

> Since the commencement of the last century when religion began to be restored from the corruptions of more than *thirteen hundred years* to something of its original purity, many treaties of theology have been published, conducted according to sounder principles, where in the chief heads of Christian doctrine are set forth sometimes briefly, sometimes in a more enlarged and methodical order.[25]

Another allusion to this can be found in *Areopagitica* in a more metaphorical style:

> Truth indeed came once into the world with her divine Master, and was a perfect shape most glorious to look upon. But when he ascended, and his apostles were laid asleep, then straight arose a wicked race of deceivers . . . who took the virgin Truth, hewed her lovely form into a thousand pieces and scattered them to the four winds.[26]

The basis for relating Milton's theological views with those of the ante-Nicean Fathers and especially Origen is an important work in Miltonic studies by Harry Robins entitled *If This be Heresy: A Study of Milton and Origen*. The thesis of this work is "the ideas which underlie the theological framework of *Paradise Lost* and the *Christian Doctrine* are far closer to those which were current among the ante-Nicean Fathers than to the orthodox conclusions of later ages."

Not much can be added here to what has been included in this work but some of the material can be collated with the objectives of this essay for purposes of clarification. The following points, then, are common to both Milton and Origen:

1. God is invisible, and inaudible, even to the Son.
2. God, the Absolute, qua God, cannot create.
3. The Word or Logos is wisdom manifested.
4. The Son achieved his place in heaven through his own merit.
5. Man dies body and soul. He remains dead until the judgement when he arises body and soul; and his body is changed into an immortal body capable of becoming one with God.
6. Christ is the second Adam.
7. God's foreknowledge in no way influenced the fall of man.[27]

Milton and Origen agree on these points through the same assumptions concerning the nature of God, Creation, and the Son. But this is not to say that Milton's orthodoxy was equally derived from various sources. For instance, while obviously differing over basic terminology and the nature of sin's effects, Milton and Augustine still agreed over the following points. It should be noted that this list is by no means exhaustive but merely representative:

1. Christ serves a functionary role between God and man as mediator.
2. Sin did not spring from Creation, but from the pride of Lucifer.
3. God gave his creatures his essence or substance only in degrees, following nature's order.
4. God foreknew that man would sin.
5. Sin came from the soul, not the flesh. Sin made flesh corruptible, not vice versa.[28]

Milton and Augustine also appear to have agreed over the nature of man's fall and the circumstances that caused it. But regardless of their common traits, all the differences between Milton and Augustine can be reduced to one essential. To Augustine, God created matter out of nothing and consequently matter tends toward evil, being radically void. For Milton, matter has been drawn from God himself and is good and divine.

Milton's thought thus blends a curious mixture of both the orthodox and the heretical. This illustrates his heavy dependence upon academic borrowing. In theology, as in politics, Milton presented his reader with the best of both worlds in a sense; the points which he held as the soundest in each particular doctrine he adopted, either fully or partially. Regardless of any consistencies that may ally him with orthodox thought, Milton's unorthodoxies are major in three respects: he was an anti-Trinitarian or subordinationist, a materialist, and a mortalist. For Milton, creation was liberation or complete freedom. The result of creation (matter) was left unrestrained to become good or evil according to the power that gave it form.[29]

III

Milton placed man in an unambiguous position in the state of nature. Regardless of the logic employed in arriving at this position, man was conceived of as completely free and capable of attaining good. But societal influences placed temptation in man's path. The ineluctable fact remains that when only two human beings existed, one caused the other's fall. Society then provided man with manifold problems. How could one achieve the good life in light of these various obstacles?: More specifically, what were the special dangers and the faculties with which to cope with them that confronted social man? Milton's answer was in general terms but nevertheless unequivocal: the prime danger was compulsion of the conscience and the faculty to combat it was right reason.

But this study has not yet arrived at Milton's commonwealth. The evidence for this can be found in his dividing of liberty into species in the *Second Defense*. This was an example of Milton's Aristotelian method. By classifying these species as the increasing quantification of the liberty of conscience from the one to the few to the many (religious, domestic, and civil), Milton drew a fine line of distinction between them. The second variety now is evident.

The argument for free speech in *Areopagitica* was simply stated: "Give me the liberty to know, to utter and to argue freely according to conscience, above all liberties."[30]

To attain the good, man as a free agent should be free of all extraneous elements which would impede his liberty. Obviously there must be some control over him to prevent anarchy and licentiousness. But this control must be personal rather than institutionally compulsive. Reliance upon personal judgement and virtue were scanty ideals in any political context, but this was Milton's answer. Here his debt to the classical republican theories becomes evident albeit he added a new dimension to the ancient paradigms; that of individualism. The best way to understand Milton's political thought is as a synthesis of classical ethical theory and republicanism along with Christian individualism.

Individual action was the precurser of political action. This was the vital element Milton retained to offset the classical conception of the *telos* of the polity. He did not quantify political action to the extent that the whole became greater than its component parts taken individually. This is not to say that the individual negated the dignity of the regime but only served to remind the political power that it was to augment the means to man's salvation, not hinder them. The true end of man was not merely political but eschatalogical. Milton's mortalism does not diminish this importance. Even if the soul dies with the body it still lies in wait for its redemption by Christ. It did not die spiritually thereby adding significant importance to the nature of

man's end on earth.
Free agency, as a gift of God, was not to be impeded by fellow man. Equally, it was dependent upon the quality of the man who possessed it. But speaking in general terms, free agency should not have to stand the test to determine the quality of the individual's will. But:

> He who is not trusted with his own actions, his drift not being known to be evil, and standing to the hazard of law and penalty, has no great argument to think himself reputed in the commonwealth wherein he was born, for other than a fool or a foreigner.[31]

Although extraneous influences may affect man's actions in a negative sense, they must not be subject to censorship by human powers since the will is assumed the final arbiter in human affairs. To the licensing problem met head on in *Areopagitica* this is evident. The higher law of nature, which books represented as symbols of man's expression and conscience, was simply not subject to the positive law. Thus, when licensing became prevalent under Archbishop Laud, the danger was clear. A distinction must be made here between licensing of this sort and censorship of a personal variety, self-imposed by the reader himself.[32] What Milton was referring to here was the legal type of censure. But any encumbrance upon the human intellect such as a licensing act or imprimatur was seen by Milton as the *reductio ad absurdum* of the proponents of such measures. The law of nature was predominant in all things. This was stated in his best metaphorical style in *Areopagitica*. Milton argued his doctrine of divorce in the same general fashion. Various factors had to be present in the conjugal bond to make it both workable and enjoyable. These factors were above the jurisdiction of earthly power; they depended entirely upon the individual relationship and exigencies which might cause its dissolution were strictly personal. Next to ignorance itself, a bad marriage was the ultimate privation the conscience could suffer.

IV

Seen in this light, Milton's denial of toleration to Catholicism was more than a personal distaste for popery. It was rooted in the doctrine of conscience delineated above. He considered heresy as ". . . a religion taken up and believed from the traditions of man and additions to the word of God." The only true heresy in Christendom was popery. The traditions of apostolic succession, papal plenitude, and the primacy of the See of Rome were all unsubstantiated by Scripture and therefore erroneous. The same was true of dogma which had crept into this tradition. In distinction to the heresy of Catholicism, Milton saw the divergent views of the various protestant denominations and sects as merely opinions based upon error. Error was merely a misunderstanding of Scripture; an act against the will. Heresy, on the other hand, was rooted in the will and a professed choice against Scripture. The Catholic church, by forbidding her members to read the Bible in their native tongues and relying rather upon the pronouncements of the papacy, substituted an "implicit" faith (believing without the authority of Scripture) for that of conscience. And since ". . . we have no warrant to regard conscience which is not grounded upon Scripture," Catholicism could simply not be tolerated.[33]

Conscience was the indirect voice of God speaking to man. Its source was Scripture, particularly the New Testament. As all Christians, Milton believed in Christ's second coming but did not emphasize this to the point that his thought became pervaded with chiliasm. Truth was apocalyptical and immutable, being merely another adjective for the wisdom of God. Man and his Creator exist in a salutary relationship; while not sharing the same essence they nevertheless complimented each other. Man derives the wisdom and reason he needs to function on earth and regain paradise while God receives the adoration of man in return. Reason was the voice and vehicle of conscience. Ontologically they were of the same essential quality but reason was given a functional definition to be applicable to the human condition. Although a natural inequality among created things predominated Milton's thought, it does not denigrate the ideal and salutary relationship that all rational beings should have with one another. In the relationship between God and man, the possibility of such a beneficial rapport was imminent, regardless of the less-than-ideal state of affairs caused by the Fall. In the conjugal tie, the relationship should again be salutary although Milton conceived of woman as inferior to man due both to the nature of her creation and the fact that she precipitated man's fall. In civil society, natural inequality again prevailed. This will be more clearly seen in the dissection of Milton's plan for a commonwealth. But this natural state did not preclude the possibility of those who participated in politics having a salutary and rational relationship. Conscience was man's natural right. Its vehicle, reason, was the fountainhead of what is called natural rights. Man without a conscience was a man in bondage to Milton; no better than a fool or slave. This is the cornerstone of

Milton's political theory.

NOTES

1. *Works*, III, pp. 37 ff.
2. *Ibid.*, pp. 153 f.
3. Hughes, p. 831.
4. *Works*, XIV, p. 25.
5. *Ibid.*, p. 63.
6. *Ibid.*, p. 81.
7. III, 118–128.
8. *Works*, XV, p. 21.
9. Lewis noted concerning this: "It is not easy to understand this doctrine, but we may note that it does not fall into the heresy against which the doctrine of creation out of nothing was intended to guard. That doctrine was directed against dualism – against the idea that God was not the sole origin of things, but found himself from the beginning faced with something other than himself. This Milton did not believe: if he has erred he has erred by flying too far from it, and believing that God made the world out of himself.", *op. cit.* p. 89.
10. *Works*, XV, p. 27.
11. *Ibid.*, pp. 47 f.
12. *Ibid.*, p. 217.
13. Messrs. W.B. Hunter and Saurat both dealt with this problem of the death of the whole man. Hunter considered death to Milton as a return to the universal order of which man and earth are seen as components of the cosmos; see "Milton's Materialistic Life Principle," *JEGP*, XLV (1946), 73. Saurat saw death in Milton's system as merely nomenclature. By delineating created things rigidly from the cosmos, he concluded that no created thing can be finally annihilated. Thus, all being is seen as immortal, see *op. cit.*, p. 119.
14. *Works*, XV, pp. 203 ff.
15. *Ibid.*, p. 113.
16. *Ibid.*, XVII, p. 5.
17. *Ibid.*, XVI, p. 153.
18. *Ibid.*, XIV, p. 181; my italics.
19. *Ibid.*, p. 189.
20. *Ibid.*, p. 231.
21. The case for Milton's Arianism, maintaining that there was no difference between the terms substance and essence in his lexicon, was made by Maurice Kelley in *This Great Argument*. It was again asserted by him in "Milton's Arianism Again Reconsidered," in the *HTR*, LIV (1961). The opposite position, claiming a semantical difference between the two terms in the text of the *Christian Doctrine*, was taken by William B. Hunter in "Some Problems in John Milton's Theological Vocabulary," also in the *HTR* LVII (1964).

22. *Works*, XV, p. 215.
23. *Ibid.*, p. 205.
24. *Ibid.*, p. 403.
25. *Ibid.*, p. 3; my italics.
26. *Hughes*, pp. 741 ff.; a more exhaustive list of quotations illustrating Milton's affinity for primitive Christianity can be found in the introduction of Robins' work.
28. These points are taken from the *City of God*, VIII, 15; X, 16; XI, 2; XI, 22; XII, 3 respectively.
29. Robins, *op. cit.*, p. 59.
30. *Hughes*, p. 746.
31. *Ibid.*, p. 735.
32. Warner Rice, "A Note on *Areopagitica*," *JEGP*, XL (1941), 477 f.
33. *Works*, VI, pp. 166 ff.

3 History and Society

Milton's conception of history was strongly influenced by a form of moral causation, i.e. by the theory that the actions of all corporeal, rational beings were predicated upon right reason. His thoughts concerning history are illustrative of this as well as a rejection of any theological determinism or fatalism. The concept of history as the enterprise by which the human mind grasped the past was free of any direct pre-determining influences. But the specific application of reason, or choice, in the public domain was not to be effected by all. Only those who possessed the greatest powers of reason were to be the caretakers of the body politic. In this way, Milton subscribed to what is commonly called a "great man" concept of history. But the art of recording events employed by him was only to make use of the positive aspects of this theory. History illustrated the possible potential of the human spirit when its rational determinants were positive. If, on the other hand, these determinants proved negative due to fallen reason, the continuum rather illustrated a tragic degradation of man's condition to what Milton conceived of as the *reductio ad nauseum* of human potential.

Two terms have been included here to help elucidate Milton's thoughts concerning history. They are "didactic experience" and a "mode of behaviour"; the latter suggested through belletristic literary forms. Both of these concepts are implied in Milton's writings and have been categorized here to clarify assumptions made from both types of his writings, the functional (political tracts) and the belletristic.

The spirit of didactic experience, while not a precise philosophic term, was explicitly mentioned by Milton in his thoughts concerning history to be the complement of untested knowledge which would have given additional credence to any postulation. It is not to be considered as a verification of an hypothesis but merely an illustration of an axiom based upon his prejudicial concept of history. Milton's historical method never presented a logical proof of an argument but rather an historical illustration to strengthen desideratum of some sort. When this method was extended to the religious field, his historical technique resembled a form of typology. At the very outset of this inquiry history must be understood to have been merely an image of Milton's bias in favor of a libertarian state. The concept of a mode of behaviour, implied through belletristic literary forms, will hopefully elucidate Milton's psychology for dealing with all estates of society in an age in which each man was considered the interpreter of his own faith. Intimation and metaphor were Milton's tools in this case. In both instances the recondite qualities of his writings will be considered as the compliments of his more explicit thought rather than being interpreted as ironic or esoteric and sufficient unto themselves.

I

Milton was not a reformer of the same caliber as his contemporaries, Dury, Hartlib, and Comenius. The universal reforms of education and philosophic systems akin to them, such as Comenius' pansophic principles, found no place in Milton's scheme of education. Neither can any democratic deductions be drawn from his principles. Milton was not an innovator for the masses but one who constructed a scheme of virtuous education which in turn was to be supported by historical writing. While granting all men freedom of conscience, a tenet of Independency, he denied democratic reform on the basis of education. The natural right of conscience, or the ability of any man to attain justice, in no way specified a system of natural political rights. Rights such as these could only be achieved through the rule of merit by a particular class of virtuous men. It was to this class that Milton addressed his historical thought. But history was not educative in an exclusive vein; it was still meant to serve a national purpose. In this latter respect, history took on the additional aspect of story-telling.

The problem that Milton's educational and political works present to the modern historian is illustrated in a specific excerpt from his *Seventh Academic Exercise (Prolusion)* presented at Cambridge. Tillyard translated it:

> So at length gentlemen, when universal *learning* has once completed its cycle, the spirit of man, no longer confined within this dark prison-house, will reach out far and wide, till it fills the whole world and space beyond with the expansion of its divine greatness.[1]

Merritt Hughes translated this same passage to read: "So at length, gentlemen, when the cycle of universal *knowledge* has been completed, still this spirit will be restless, . . . etc."² The problem presented by the terms *knowledge* and *learning* in the above context is more than a simple, semantical one. Milton defined learning as the efficient cause of knowledge, vividly illustrating the epistemological difference between the two terms. In this case, universal knowledge was not denied since it was intricately bound to God. But universal learning is a more tenuous term in Milton's vocabulary. It must be understood as a regenerative process, but not manifest through any particular means. Milton's educational plan was not a realization of either concept but merely the functional basis of his political theory. He never denied access to universal knowledge but it found no specific manifestation in his thought.

The importance which Milton attributed to education was,

. . . to repair the ruins of our first parents by regaining to know God aright, and out of that knowledge to love Him, to imitate Him, to be like Him, as we may the nearest by possessing our souls of true virtue.³

The close relationship of education, religion, and freedom of conscience reveals the immediate nature of Milton's social proposals and casts light upon the gravity with which he held these particular ideas, which were later to provide the ontological basis of the state.

The source of educational reform was naturally children but there were aspects of a proper education which children could not fully appreciate until they achieved a certain age and training, viz. admiration of the virtuous and the noble. The commonwealth should be imbued with the proper civic virtues when the citizens are young but equally must be nurtured in a continuing process. Such was the organic nature of education. History's role in education was similar; nurture of the virtuous and noble. It is ancillary to education in Milton's plan which is itself ministerial to the commonweath. To illustrate this, Milton steeped the origins of political community, like Rousseau, in the state of pre-political society. While Milton gave an extraordinary account of human progress, it was consistent with his overall conception of reform.

Learning was Milton's vehicle for the redress of oppression. The evolution of the arts and sciences underlayed the development of civilization. Before civilized society developed, learning played little or no part in those human relationships which were to become the rudiments of political community; "the sound of the cithara was not heard." With the advancement of learning, the arts and sciences inspired,

> ... the rude breasts of men, imbued them with the knowledge of themselves and induced them to live within common walls ... if we go back to ancient times, we shall find that commonwealths were not disciplined, but founded upon learning.[4]

Since the educational spirit or experience was not considered a product of social progress but anterior, or at least coeval with society itself, its distinctive role as the *sine qua non* of Milton's thought comes to the surface. Politics appears only as a necessary evil; a possible guide to the good life. The learning process, however, does not evolve from such negative circumstances. It was intricately woven into the natural right of man as a positive element; his vehicle of redress and attainment of justice.

Milton's contemporary period was one of a potential new dawn after centuries of what he considered stagnation and his contemporary milieu reflected a continuation of this absurdity to an extent. The last vestiges of Scholasticism particularly came under attack from him. As early as his university tenure at Cambridge his thought was strongly rejecting the "bog of sophistry—that art which the Aristotelians call metaphysics." Legal science fared no better and suffered from the "... confusion of our system and still worse from a jargon I can hardly tell how to describe. It may be the gibberish of American Indians and it may not be human speech at all."[5]

Viewed with political connotations, this concept of his contemporary society was highly charged with a revolutionary aspect which has been all but overlooked. It was also pervaded with apolitical connotations as well. This distinction reverts back to his ethics and the role of conscience as the primary force in religion and politics. With such an ethical orientation in mind, Milton was able to maintain the Aristotelian formula for happiness as the true end of the commonwealth:

> For if it be a higher point of wisdom in every private man, much more is it in a nation, to know itself rather than puffed up with vulgar flatteries, and encomiums, for want of self-knowledge, to enterprise rashly and to come off miserably in great undertakings.[6]

To enable the commonwealth to do so as a whole:

History and Society

To make the people fittest to choose and the chosen fittest to govern will be to mend our corrupt and faulty education.[7]

As will be seen later, the "chosen" here were not merely the successful candidates of a ballot.

The statesman, upon whom the ultimate happiness of the commonwealth depended, could have found a practical value in a type of history designed to compliment this end. The role of a national history was to teach one the nature of his fellow countrymen and by comparing past and present, to raise ". . . knowledge of ourselves both great and weighty, and judge what we are to achieve." Incompetence on a national level was tantamount to diverting the true end of the commonwealth and imposing a "yoke" upon it through ignorance. This was the type of continuum that Milton saw as capriciously subjecting mankind since the Fall. The reform of education, ". . . one of the greatest and noblest designs that can be thought on and for want thereof this nation perishes," was the instrument designed to break this continuum.

History's usefulness is still elliptical since two elements need to be examined; the quality of the historian and the nature of the audience for whom he wrote. Both characteristics aid in determining whether the history will be a true one in Milton's sense or merely a "monkish gloss" upon historical writing:

> This, then, is my view: that he who would write of worthy deeds worthily must write with mental endowments and experience of affairs not less than were in the doer of the same, so as to be able with equal mind to comprehend and measure even the greatest of them, and, when he has comprehended them, to relate them distinctly and gravely in pure and chaste speech.[8]

The elements of nobility and virtue in history tend to place it in the caliber of the heroic and at the same time make it somewhat ironic, in that it will be incomprehensible to those who do not possess or recognize the qualities portrayed. However, this type of person could still have benefited from the simpler story-telling aspects. Both the method and effect of history provide the key to Milton's historical thought. One cannot exist without the other since both were components of a desired effect.

Milton's historical method was illustrative of this. History was not merely rhetoric or persuasive speech and this was suggested in its style: ". . . that he should do so in an ornate style, I do not much care about; for I want a Historian, not an Orator."⁹ By drawing a fine line of distinction between the functions of rhetoric and history, Milton illustrated that he was fully aware of the differences between the two disciplines based upon their classical origins. With the persuasive element in a subordinate role, the reader can at least grasp what history was not. Combined with the experience of the historian, history took on an aura of pure didacticism. Virtue was fused with experience in order to introduce a practical element into the noble. Milton's distaste for purely speculative matters required a modicum of action or practicality to be introduced to the theoretical. Experience was one of the true elements of a good education. But base or ignoble types were to be discounted. Thus, experience must be drawn from a source potentially didactic, i.e. virtuous, and not merely real, worldly, or base.

II

The closest approximation to the immanentization of knowledge in society was political action—virtuous political action. Due to man's fallen nature the once Christian end of mankind was immediately replaced by the conventional in the form of the Christian commonwealth. Milton did not see this as incongruous. The Christian commonwealth possessed the potential to be a terrestrial city of God meeting both the spiritual and worldly needs of its citizens. The two realms were to reconcile themselves through faith and love. However, since by its nature and origin political society was essentially base, it required a social force compatible with the Christian which would equally embrace Christian ideals. Milton conceived of this force as virtuous action; a compliment of the virtue of faith. This was the spirit of education, no more than the institutionalized manifestation of this force. It was best evidenced in Christ's reply to Satan in *Paradise Regained*:

> Think but that I know these things; or think
> I know them not; not therefore am I short
> Of knowing what I ought; he who receives
> Light from above, from the fountain of light,
> No other doctrine needs.[10]

Knowledge was not an instrument which needed any outward sign to augment itself. It was complete and self-sufficient. But mankind did need an apotheosis of political action which would have been directly comprehensible to the imperfect state of wordly affairs, or a mode of behaviour. Virtuous action, as the manifestation of faith and love, suggested this mode of behaviour to political man to keep him in line. Milton's apparent denigration of untested knowledge in the human sphere was not vacillation. It was in keeping with this somewhat vague idea of action enhanced by experience. Virtue was objective as well as nominative and Milton's use of history was concerned with both cases. The problem stated in *Paradise Regained* as:

> However, many books
> Wise men have said are wearisome: who reads
> Incessantly and to his reading brings not
> A spirit and judgement equal or superior
> (And what he brings, what he needs elsewhere seek)
> Uncertain and unsettl'd still remains
> Deep verst in books and shallow in himself.[11]

was best succinctly summed up in the *Christian Doctrine*: "Not the hearers of the law but the doers of the law shall be justified."

Three of Milton's favourite characters illustrate this emphasis on action. In the political realm, Milton's erstwhile hero was Cromwell. Milton had a specific conception of ruler in mind and Cromwell filled it as well as any major statesman of the day. The Protector's qualities earned him the highest accolades of Milton's esteem: ". . . we all willingly yield the palm of sovereignty to your unrivalled ability and virtue."[12] Cromwell achieved this by displaying the proper balance in state relations; that between peace and war: ". . . when we found, though not for the first time, that you were as wise in the cabinet as valiant in the field."[13] Cromwell was able to comprehend liberty and its exigencies by having virtuously fought for it and provided a specific example of nobility fused with experience. He was an historical figure of heroic proportions and a prime example of Milton's idea of the balanced individual.

The dubious hero of *Paradise Lost* was also one who learned by experience. Adam possessed all the knowledge and potential that mankind would ever be capable of prior to the Fall and yet did not realize it until an act caused him to lose it.[14] This experience and the insight into what he had wrought upon posterity was followed by his famous utterance in Book XII of *Paradise Lost*:

> Light out of darkness! full of doubt I stand

> Whether I should repent me now of sin
> By mee done and occasion'd, or rejoice
> Much more, that much more good thereof shall spring.

Adam's *felix culpa* was that of attaining human knowledge and with it, political wisdom. This wisdom was derived from the original sin and its concomitant lust. Society as it is known had its origins in sin and concupiscence. This is not a delineation of the origins of society to the point of supererogation. Rather than positing a primevil state after the manner of Hobbes, Milton adopted the Fall story as the pivotal point in human destiny. By disobeying God, Adam in turn provided mankind with a new precept; not to act as a surrogate for faith, but rather to compliment it in the ruin left after the initial act of disobedience. But man was not capable of following a precept of theoretical proportions in regard to faith, as the original disobedience showed. It follows, then, that the same would be true of any precept based upon his own theoretical wisdom. Since the actions of the will were initially based upon the power of reason but could in fact become divorced from it. Milton naturally attributed the training of both faculties a prominent role in his social philosophy. While reason was equated with theoretical wisdom, the will was related to the emotions and Milton regarded the training of the emotions as well as the training of reason as significant. Thus, education in part had to rely upon an emotional effect to control the appetitive desires.[15]

The drama is illustrative of the technique that was closest to Milton's dictum concerning the writing of history. As history involved the virtue of the writer it equally involved the virtue of the reader to whom it was supposed to have proved didactic. Milton's drama amplified this theme. The introduction to *Samson Agonistes* stated:

> Tragedy, as it was anciently composed, hath ever been held the gravest, moralest and most profitable of all other poems: therefore said by Aristotle to be of the power by raising pity and fear, or terror, to purge the mind of those and such like passions.[16]

Tragedy ministers to the audience while involving the virtue of the author and was similar to history in this respect. Both art forms attempt an elevation of man's dignity; tragedy to the extent that man's reach over-extends his competence, making his fall inevitable. Both forms achieve an elevation but history does so purely through a display of virtue in Milton's plan. Comedy is excluded here because it portrays man lower in dignity than is his nature thereby emphasising the ignoble.

The true difference between history and tragedy is based upon an Aristotelian distinction. By raising pity and fear to catharsis, tragedy ministers to the emotional part of the soul. It would not be incorrect to say that history cannot achieve the same effect but the motive and procedure of writing each is quite different. Tragedy was able to take allowances that Milton would never have permitted history. Following Aristotle's suggestion in the *Poetics* (1451b 7) in *Samson Agonistes*, Milton created a fictional character to add to the biblical (Harapha), forced recognition and denouement through the chorus, and raised catharsis through Samson's self-immolation (following 1452b 4). History possessed an honesty which would not permit this method. Its characters must have been genuine and the method of recording their actions must have been free of any psychological device. One form raised pity and fear, the other "conceptions" based upon virtuous action. The didactic value of each art form was to be measured by the reaction it aroused in the reader or viewer. In Aristotle's sense, it is hard to imagine a purely didactic literary tragedy since it would have to appeal to the emotions to be an actual tragedy which would in turn preclude it from being instructive in a strict sense. It may be said that the time element brings out the most succinct difference between the two forms. While tragedy was concerned with the effect of passions, history was rather concerned with the recording of these passions and their eventual outcome through the narrative.

In a political context, Milton was suggesting a mode of behaviour in his use of both of these art forms. For those already possessing the quality of virtue, he was advocating nurture of that quality. The story of Samson is an example. Besides advocating nurture of virtue by illustrating its very opposite, it instructed the unlearned that to sin was to earn death. In the latter case, it does so through simple storytelling. History did the same but in the former case it aroused the noble spirit rather than the passions. This type of "rational purgation" was in keeping with the entire framework of Milton's ideas of natural law and the constant submission of the appetitive soul. It would appear that it was not mere coincidence when Milton advocated in *Of Education*: ". . . when all these other employments are well conquered, then will the choice histories, heroic poems, and Attic tragedies . . . offer themselves."

III

Milton's political activities interrupted his *History of Britain* and quite possibly retarded its conclusion. By 1649, four of the six books were completed and published with the entire version appearing in 1670. The period of its composition spanned most of his literary career. A predominant theme of the work is one which appeared throughout most of his work in either a polemical, literary, or historical form—the "yoke" concept. This yoke took many forms in his works. It was probably best described in spirit in the *History of Britain* as the ". . . long suffering of God (which) permits bad men to enjoy prosperous days with the good, so his severity oft times exempts not good men from their share in evil times with the bad."[17] This was reiterated in *Paradise Lost*:

> Therefore since hee permits
> Within himself unworthy powers to reign
> Over free reason, God in judgement just
> Subjects him from without to violent lords.[18]

The yoke was a direct product of imprudent spirit; a submission or improper subjection of the conscience. Wherever and in whatever form it appeared, the idea of inward liberty was initially involved. The didactic quality of the *History of Britain* was an illustration of this.

Milton's history ended with the Norman invasion of 1066. Even if it was the author's intention to proceed no further, which is unlikely, it still portrayed the yoke explicitly. Prior to the invasion, the state of English society was, according to Milton, in a state of decay. The clergy was largely responsible for this state of affairs: "the monks went did in fine stuffs and made no difference what they eat." Regardless of their various drawbacks, monks were the best historians of their age and Milton gave them credit for it. They added a positive contribution to the age with their scholarship; Bede being the best of them. The advent of William the Conquerer was seen as the "just severity" of God, who only subjected men to outward tyranny which complimented the already present inward. The Norman conquest completed the cycle of the full gamut of servitude and provided total tyranny. Unfortunately, Milton never explicitly mentioned whether or not the servitude had ever been successfully broken.

In his systematic political works, as well as in his two histories, there was less mention of religious influence than in his more polemical diatribes. As C. H. Firth pointed out, no mention was made of bishops in the *History of Britain*.[19] And in his educational treatise, religious education played a subordinate role to classical studies. This was not a sin of omission on Milton's part. While religious influences had a valuable polemical quality in debate, their position in serious inquiry was another matter. Since history was to aim at a virtuous objectivity, religion and its concomitant polemical fervor were to be kept subdued. This was also evident in Milton's treatment of moral choice in *Of Education*. By using the concept of *proairesis* in its strict Aristotelian context, the subjective nature of religious influence was omitted in favor of the classical concept of decision based upon right reason alone. The study of things political needed right reason to be set aright but religion was rather a matter purely of conscience, and faith which did not require serious dialectical inquiry.

Climatological conditions and geography also played a role in Milton's historical thought:

> The study of geography is both profitable and delightful; but the writers thereof, though some of them exact enough in setting down longitudes and latitudes, yet in those other relations of manners, religion, government, and such-like, accounted geographical, have for the most part missed their proportions . . . which perhaps brought into the mind of some learned men and judicious, who had not the leisure or purpose to write an entire geography, yet at least to assay something in the description of one or two countries.[20]

The idea of an universal history or geography was not rejected, but the leisure usually needed to write a good one was the ultimate problem. If this was the case with history, it would appear to have been no different with an universal, educational scheme.

Milton wrote for the English national character and no other. Any educational scheme designed for any portion of the population would have to take this political aspect into account. The introduction to the *History of Muscovy* showed the same affinity:

> I began with Muscovy, being the most northern region of the earth purported civil and the most northern parts thereof first discovered by English voyagers.

This penchant was more than mere chauvinism. It exemplified the reforming spirit needed to set political affairs aright.

The concept of didactic experience is by its nature a solecism if implied within a context of universal appeal. In the same manner, it severely limited those who may have benefited by it or participated in virtuous action. This is equally true of the other synthetic term employed in this essay. A mode of behaviour suggested that the end in mind must have been recognizable or appealing to the individual. In antithesis, the Christian element in Milton's thought would have possibly posited a universal system by its transcendental nature but more likely it was no more than a technical device of his language and thought. It is impossible to denigrate the role of religion in Milton but one can say with some assurance that its pietistic nature played a lesser role in his thought than the purely philosophical aspects of moral inquiry.

History was an indeterminate discipline to Milton if his reader accepts his disparate thoughts on the subject at face value. It is easier to say what history was not than what it actually symbolized. It did not signify a philosophy as such any more than it represented a world cycle culminating in the Reformation. Besides some polemical material to the contrary, there is nothing to substantiate such a view in his prose. What it was is quite another matter. That it was moral, representative, and potentially didactic has been illustrated. But the illustrations have in themselves been scarce. If this fact suggests nothing else, it does point out that history as Milton conceived of it was part of a much larger system in his thought which was better defined. In relation to the conscience, it was a vehicle of experience as well as a paradigm for posterity. Thus, its nature was basically heuristic. It formed a part of the mechanistic process of Milton's simple psychology which placed the burden of all action squarely upon the individual. It represented only a small, but nevertheless, significant part of the efficient cause of political society—acquisite wisdom. Its true importance lay in the fact that it represented a moral pattern of conduct, both in recording events and in determining their cause, which administered to a higher good or end. It implied a refutation (which was more explicit in his other works) to non-rational determinism and chance and vividly showed that the efficient cause of society was not dependent upon fortuitous circumstances. If history displayed any qualities which would be deemed universal it did so only in an indirect manner. While it could symbolize the universal truth, the emphasis was always upon the subjunctive.

NOTES

1. Phyllis Tillyard (trans.), *John Milton: Private Correspondence and Academic Exercises* (Cambridge, 1932); my italics.

2. *Hughes*, p. 625; my italics.
3. *Ibid.*, p. 631.
4. *Ibid.*, p. 624.
5. *Ibid.*, p. 627.
6. *Works*, X, p. 103; also Aristotle, *Ethics*, 1194b 8–10 and 1195a 14–16.
7. *Hughes*, p. 891.
8. *Works*, XII, p. 93.
9. *Ibid.*, pp. 93 f.
10. IV, 286–90.
11. IV, 321–27.
12. *Works*, VIII, p. 223.
13. *Ibid.*
14. The concept of the potentiality of man prior to the Fall is examined in A.J. Waldock, *Paradise Lost and Its Critics* (Cambridge, 1964), p. 27; J.N.D. Kelly, *Early Christian Doctrines* (London, 1958), p. 362; and Norman P. Williams, *The Ideas of the Fall and of Original Sin* (London, 1929), pp. 362 ff.
15. See M.W. Bundy, "Milton's View of Education in Paradise Lost," *JEGP*, XX1 (1922), 149.
16. This is better known as the power of homeopathic purgation, or "like purges like." It was classified in the same manner by G.E. Lessing in the *Hamburg Dramaturgy*, trans. H. Zimmern (New York, 1962), pp. 186 ff.
17. *Works*, X, p. 316.
18. XII, 90–93.
19. C.H. Firth, "Milton as Historian," *Proceedings of the British Academy*, III (1907).
20. *Works*, X, p. 327.

4 Education

In the preceding chapter it was determined that Milton wrote for two types of audience. The elitism which is implicit in his historical thought is quite explicit in his tractate *Of Education*. The true nature of Milton's thought is reflected in this brief and succinct tract. Education can be said to serve the same twofold purpose as history. However, as in the story-telling aspects of history, Milton was purposely elliptical in the secondary nature of education. While history served a functional purpose with respect to the unlearned by suggesting a mode of behaviour, education concerned itself only with those who possessed the potential to achieve a proper degree of virtue and grace. Its secondary characteristics were only implied. *Of Education* is typical of all his works in general; it was addressed to a select few. His opening remark in the *Doctrine and Discipline of Divorce* was typical of this:

> I seek not to seduce the simple and illiterate; my errand is to find out the choicest and learnedst, who have this high gift of wisdom to answer solidly, or to be convinced.[1]

Milton, as a political writer, deemed all experience in life as a didactic part of civil deportment. Obviously, when he went seeking precedents for his thought he reverted to the classical authors whose authority was not in doubt. This type of academic *stare decisis* led Milton to a typically classical ethical conclusion; pleasure is not an end in itself but only a subordinate part of a greater whole, the common good. All of his writings in some respect reflect this trend. His pamphlets and parliamentary tracts all have one common end, praise of the commonwealth. But since the state was only as virtuous as its members, Milton directed his protean literary abilities at the nurture of these ideals. The tract on education is central to this and basic to all of his other political writings.

Of Education presents the reader with labyrinthine problems due to its content. Over forty-five authors and numerous works were cited by Milton as its origins and content in the brief eight or so pages that the work comprised. Regardless of these numerous origins, ". . . three authorities are discernible in Milton's beliefs; nature, the Bible, and the writings of certain men outside the Bible."[2] While noting these other influences education was primarily concerned with the last of these three influences as the vehicle to the use of right reason. This differentiated Milton from Comenius. In his *Reformation of Schooles*, an abridged version of his *Didactica*, Comenius stated his two sources or authorities:

> Therefore, the rules whereby our pansophy is to be erected, must be borrowed from these two, Nature and Scripture, whereby all things great and final, high and low, first and last, visible, created and uncreated, may be reduced to such an Harmony (or Pan-harmony rather) as which is true, perfect, and every way complete, and satisfactory to itself, and to things themselves.[3]

Comenius planned to take the disparate writings of numerous authors and synthesize them into a relevant scheme which he termed pansophy. Needless to say, this would not have appealed to Milton. The classics stood by themselves and not as Comenius held: "Therefore the precepts of Pansophy ought to contain nothing in them, but what is worth our serious knowledge."[4] The uniqueness of Milton's thought in this tract is its traditional approach in an era which was moving strongly in the direction of universal and pragmatic goals. No attempt has been made here to deal with all of these authors, but only the major ones who directly influenced his thought—notably Plato and Aristotle. This has been done because the tract is essentially political and its true significance is in its political connotations. However, regardless of these political connotations, it is still in the tradition of better educational thought. The political aspects of this, as well as any educational theory, can be attributed to one factor which transcends the traditional, disciplinary boundaries—experience. Cheyney Culpeper, a member of Hartlib's circle and an activist in educational reform, wrote to Hartlib in 1645:

> I pray' (as you shall have the opportunity) inform your selfe of the choice on which a schollar may be with Mr. Milton, that . . . I may satisfy such with whome (till he be more knowne) that consideration is like to weigh. There are some good sprinklings in his (as I conceive it to be) letter of Education, but (under favor I conceive) there is not descending enough into particulars, but rather a general notion of what experience only can perfect.[5]

I

Milton's theory of education combined an Aristotelian framework with elements of Platonism to form this elitist approach to learning. In the first instance, Milton used Aristotle's three means of education, natural endowment, formation of habit, and cultivation of the rational principle within, as set forth in the *Politics*, and complimented them with the functional aspects of such an education as expounded by Plato in the *Laws*. This type of education was to nurture the greater whole, the common good of the commonwealth. By this method Milton also excluded the type of man that he held the most contempt for; the professional politician or courtier, who used politics for personal gain or recognition. Milton's commonwealth was to depend upon the cultivated gentleman to provide its sustenance. With his marked antipathy to the monarchy and the court, it was natural that his educational process would include those studies designed to inculcate one with virtues he felt were lacking in the monarchical form of government.

The Aristotelian formula that the regime's educational process should be compatible with its end and therefore unitary was wholeheartedly in agreement with Milton's commonwealth. However, in considering Milton as the educationalist élitist that he was, a difficulty arises in this theory. If, as he ostensibly claimed, the education of the commonwealth was to be the same for all, how could all participate in the political process if this education was geared for the exceptionally bright and studious child? When he proposed education on a national scale it brought out this glaring distinction of an exclusively run republic based upon an exclusive education. But democratic logic was not a part of Milton's thought. Naturally, since all members of the commonwealth did not have the ability to comprehend a Miltonic curriculum, a majority of them would be excluded from the political processes of integration and participation. Milton did not state that he ever intended to design a commonwealth quantitatively different from that of Britain under the monarchy so he must be taken at his word and utopian plans must be discounted. The answer to this problem lies in a close examination of *Of Education*. Then his educational theory will also provide some insight into his ideas concerning political participation.

Numerous schools of educational reformers were active during this period, the Comenians being the most renowned. While advocating a

Education 55

reform of education along pansophic lines, as expounded by Comenius, they did share a common goal with Milton who was otherwise opposed, or at least apathetic, to them. This was a dissatisfaction with ideal societies. As will be shown later, this feeling of futility towards utopias was essentially Milton's as well. Perhaps the common bond of all seventeenth century educational reformers was best stated by Hartlib in his preface to Dury's *Reformed School*:

> Therefore, to meddle with the multitudes of the aged people (the Objects of their charges) who are now settl'd and habituated in the way of their own choosing, if to think to draw from it, is to attempt *without discretion*, an impossibilitie... it followeth that there is none other way left but to deal with the young ones, before any corrupt habits, and perverse engagements be confirmed upon them.[6]

Milton wrote his tractate in English rather than in Latin. This style is suggestive of two things. First, by using the vernacular he was proving to be consistent in his plan for national reform. One would not have used Latin to appeal primarily to Englishmen concerning the reform of a British institution. Secondly, by doing so he took himself out of the company of the universal reformers who used Latin as their vehicle for universal recognition. But this was not always the case with Milton. When he engaged in the pamphlet war with Salamasius his rebuttals were written in Latin (*Defense of the English People*). Both editions of *Of Education* (1644 and 1673) appeared in English; the first as a letter to Hartlib and the other in a collection of poems.

As has been previously shown in his evolution of learning, Milton's particular bias was that the arts and sciences, *inter alia*, were functional and to an extent, self-sufficient. Milton's concept of human progress was based upon this academic bias that the arts were coeval with the advance of society. The arts provided Milton with a sense of tradition, even more so than religious or civil institutions. His discussion of education conspicuously omitted the first of Aristotle's three means (natural endowment) as understood. This particular factor was intrinsic to mankind, or supposed to have been. Milton appears not to have recognised the plenitude of human capabilities; men were either learned or illiterate. In his discussion of education he began with the second of Aristotle's means, the formation of habit, and embodied it in the curriculum of his proposed academy.

The brevity of the tract was by design rather than by accident. Nevertheless, the need for action was evident in the opening paragraph to Hartlib: "Brief I shall endeavor to be; for that which I have to say, assuredly this nation hath extreme need should be done sooner than spoken." His rejection of the tedious and lengthy works of Comenius appears to have been an attempt toward brevity as well as a return to the classical theories rather than striving to found an innovative one. The uniqueness of Milton's thought is not to be found in innovation but rather in his extraordinary grasp of the Greek and Latin classics which formed his basic curriculum.

Before proceeding into Milton's tract one point should be kept in mind as one studies these far-ranging ideas. It would not be an incorrect assumption, based upon evidence already presented, that Milton's *Of Education* forms a sort of preamble to the government proposed in his *Commonwealth* much in the same way that Jowett classified the books of Plato's *Laws* concerning education as a preamble to the proposed regime of Crete in the subsequent books. The purpose of such a method would be essentially ethical in that only a man properly educated in civic virtue would acquiesce to the laws of the state. In Milton's case education, then, was an intrinsic part of liberty. This argument may at first appear to proceed *non sequitor*, but this is not the case. Milton attempted to legitimize the relationship between ruler and ruled by basing it upon ethical grounds. By doing so he attempted to maintain individual liberty in its proper perspective. As was seen earlier, education was a part of that triad of domestic liberty which included the conjugal tie and the free publication of thoughts. His doctrines of divorce and free speech were famous for their championship of individual liberty against compulsion, whether to the state or to a marriage partner and the church. In education Milton stated this championship more subtlety. After the attainment of a decent knowledge of Latin ". . . some other hour of the day might be taught the rules of arithmetic and soon after the element of geometry, even playing as the old manner was." This was a reiteration of Socrates caveat in the *Republic*:

> Enforced exercise does no harm to the body, but enforced learning will not stay in the mind. So avoid compulsion and let your child's lessons take the form of play. This will also help you to see what they are naturally fitted for.[7]

Milton was not urging laxity or under-emphasizing the strenuous mental activity of a child's learning process but simply urging a sensible approach to these vigors.

In *Of Education* Milton defined the end of learning as follows:

To repair the ruins of our first parents by regaining to know God aright, and out of that knowledge to love him, to imitate him, to be like him, as we may the nearest by possessing our souls of true virtue, which being united to the heavenly grace of faith makes up the highest perfection.

Now the "ruins of our first parents" may be defined through various political or religious techniques. In this case we shall define it as the loss of right reason. By striving to regain the potential and knowledge of Adam in its proper perspective, Milton attributed education the chief place in his social thought. But this was not to be achieved by grasping in the darkness or by involving abstract principles, it was to be done with a knowledge of "sensible" things. This knowledge of the practical added civility to mankind, or what Aristotle called felicity. This was the epitomy of knowledge, its practical manifestation.

This knowledge of sensible things was initially illustrated in the study of languages:

And seeing every nation affords not experience and tradition enough for all kinds of learning, therefore we are chiefly taught the languages of those people who have at any time been most industrious after wisdom.

Words and lexicons were not enough in this respect, the "solid" things in languages must be emphasized, i.e. what the language symbolized as well as what it stated. The basic element of Milton's education was Latin in particular. A working knowledge of Latin was a prerequisite to the reading of the more difficult texts and would also shorten the previously agonizing and long process of a difficult curriculum and instruction.[8] But Latin itself had to be purged of its medieval elements and returned to its purist classical form. Milton advocated the removal of such difficulties in his little-known *Accedence Commenced Grammar*, published in 1669. Hartlib also proposed the same in the *True and Readie Way to Learn the Latin Tongue*, 1645. But to use the principle that Dury used later in attempting to explain language instruction would probably have been merely repetitious in Milton's mind. In the *Reformed School* Dury claimed that the acquisition of a working knowledge of the vernacular was a prerequisite to the learning of Latin. The same was true of Comenius' propositions in the *Didactica*. However, it was not until Latin had been purged that a good education could be commenced.

Before Milton began his discourse upon education he digressed into a lengthy diatribe against the errors of teaching in the universities and the products of his contemporary educational process. For whatever reason Milton may personally have disliked the method of teaching in the universities, his reasoning and method of beginning instruction with the "arts most easy" and proceeding to the more difficult studies was quite sound. But the sophistry he described after this was more than polemics. Although ostensibly swiping at the doctrine of absolute monarchy in that; "tyrannous aphorisms appear to them the high points of wisdom; instilling their hearts with a conscientious slavery," Milton was calling for a return to right reason. He was at one with Plato in urging the emphasis of the superior rather than the inferior in men's souls, i.e. the rule of the best within man. Rather than instilling first principles in their matriculates, education institutions were rather inculcating them with pleasure sought as an end in itself. The Platonic tripartite division of essences will help in later explicating Milton's ideas.

II

Milton began his tractate proper in a peripatetic fashion with strong overtones of the Platonic theory of ideas:

> I shall detain you no longer in the demonstration of what we should not do, but straight conduct ye to a hillside where I will point ye out the right path of a virtuous and noble education; laborious indeed at the first ascent, but else so smooth, so green, so full of goodly prospect and melodious sounds on every side.

This was a paraphrase of the Athenian Stranger's quote from Hesiod in the *Laws*:

> But before virtue the immortal gods have placed the sweat of labour, and long and steep is the way thither, and rugged at first; but when you have reached the top, although difficult before, it is then easy.[9]

Milton was attempting to lead Hartlib out of the world of opinion into that of knowledge. He assumed the role of a voyager, a Socrates or a Raphael Hythloday; one who has seen or known a better life. This element of play in Milton was used to underscore the gravity of the topic he was about to explicate. Milton's eventual rejection of utopian schemes will add even more gravity to the ensuing proposals. But unlike an utopian voyager, Milton gives his reader the impression that he was not a stranger or a visitor to this new world, but an inhabitant. The reader must, then, accept his thoughts as perfectly serious. No other form of education could provide a man with "that which fits a man to perform justly, skillfully and magnanimously all the offices, both public and private, of peace and war." Allegorically, a statesman could only lead others up the laborious ascent after he himself had seen the sun and returned. Milton was never specific in describing how Cromwell achieved his esteem. But, as will be seen later, Milton had another hero figure in mind who approached this idea of wisdom personified. This virtuous inculcation was to be accomplished between the ages of twelve and twenty-one.

The academy was to be a self-sufficient unit:

> First, to find out a spacious house and ground about it fit for an academy and big enough to lodge a hundred and fifty persons, whereof twenty or thereabout may be attendants all under the government of one . . . this place should be at once, both school and university, not needing to remove to any other house of scholarship.[10]

Dury made the same remarks in his *Reformed School*. Obviously, Milton felt that more could be assimilated without the bother of changing locations, as his own Horton period reflected. This type of academy was to be established in "every city throughout the land, which would tend much to the increase of learning and civility everywhere." This was only to be a nation-wide program in a very general sense. The education of women was excluded as well as that of the lower economic and social strata.

Milton divided his plan into three parts, analagous to a day's labour; studies, exercise, and diet. The studies or curriculum included those disciplines which would give the student a "tincture of natural knowledge." After these preliminaries, which Milton did not specify in length of time, he introduced the pivotal issue in his entire social theory—the attainment of *proairesis* or moral choice. After the attainment of this indispensible tool the more difficult disciplines were presented; economics, politics, religion, poetry, tragedy and the organic arts. This was to be followed by a second division, the exercise of these studies. This was to be the procedural method of carrying out these various disciplines. Lastly, Milton briefly mentioned the "diet." These three divisions form the basis of his educational theory.

The tripartite division of learning in Milton's tract closely coincides with the tripartite division of essences as expounded by Plato in the *Laws*. For a moment, let us substitute Milton's education for Plato's essence while letting its division equal Plato's name and definition. By paraphrasing this section of the *Laws* Milton's plan can be considered in this way. "Sometimes a person may give the name and ask the definition or he may give the definition and ask the name; both times arriving at the same essence."[11] "Studies" (curriculum) is capable of being divided into two parts (for the sake of example) languages and classical authors. This is the definition of education. Conversely, languages and classical studies are called or named "studies." By giving the name and asking the definition or by giving the definition and asking the name, one is still speaking of the same thing. While probably not doing justice to Plato, this analogy helps elucidate Milton's thought quite clearly. Regardless of the name that Milton gave a thing, he was still speaking of the same essence. His education in itself was an essence; its name (curriculum) and definition being simply other means of expressing the same. On a higher level of abstraction this type of relation remains the same. If the essence is considered as a virtuous man, his definition as educated, and his name as gentleman, it becomes obvious that the individual is the pillar of Milton's social philosophy. Regardless of the level of abstraction used in considering essence, its name and definition will correspond proportionately to that particular essence. Simply, Milton's theory can be boiled down ontologically to a simple factor which never became obfuscated even in his more advanced social ideas. The role of studies particularly is crucial in this scheme since it contained the element of *proairesis*, which was the primary cognitive essence in human affairs.

The pivotal point in Milton's tract marks the maturity of the student. The concept of moral choice was best defined by Aristotle as a voluntary action based upon a preference. Choice does not depend upon opinion because it is made concerning things which are known about while opinions are formed about things not known about. It is based upon knowledge of some sort. This was the concept Milton used; the classical idea of *proairesis*. The mark of a virtuous man was not a relative thing to Milton but rather an absolute quality. As there could be no relativism between good and evil, neither could there be any concerning a man's actions. Since choice was a voluntary action the one who took the particular action was to be held fully responsible for it, because it was intricately based upon his character and will. Choice was given to man through his reason and remains as his sole instrument to distinguish him from the lower forms of life. "Many there be that complain of divine providence for suffering Adam to transgress. Foolish tongues! when God gave him reason, he gave him freedom to choose, for reason is but choosing."[12] Since man was the sole agent of his fate and reason was the vehicle of that fate, Milton would not accept any plan which did not exploit man's individual abilities and liberty to the utmost.

In advocating this specific type of education, Milton refused to be led into the *cul de sac* that Thomas More and Plato found themselves in with regard to their idealistic proposals. His quarrel with utopian plans had a functional tone.

> To sequester out of the world into Atlantic and Utopian politics, which never can be drawn into use, will not mend our condition, but to ordain wisely as in this world of evil, in the midst whereof God hath placed us unavoidably.[13]

Milton fully agreed with Plato that youth must be guided toward right reason but differed substantially in the method. His strong sense of Christian individualism showed itself here. Through his "realistic" approach to education and society, Milton was preparing youth to be able to stand alone as Adam did in choosing between the two forces in the world. He did not accept Plato's argument that men are the puppets of the gods and that the string they cling to is the cord of reason. But neither did he totally reject it. While agreeing in principle with Plato that an unmoved mover was the primary cause of all causes, Milton was still able to maintain a sense of individual political liberty without the aid or intervention of the gods. His real argument with the Platonic tradition concerned the licensing of certain acts by the state for the supposed common good. Milton's attempt to free man from the strictures of the Platonic commonwealth did not require statutory regulation. Right reason properly nurtured would obviate any need for civil restrictions upon the actions of the individual citizen.

Milton and Plato appear to be coming to an impasse concerning the use of compulsion in the process of acquisite wisdom, both within and without the formal educational scheme. But it is unlikely that Milton was accusing Plato of totalitarian tactics. It appears that he was attacking the language in which the *Laws* were written. Milton was taken back by the reversion to a scheme which most readers would generally misunderstand. It would be equally difficult to comprehend him agreeing with Plato over substance and differing over procedure. Milton's championship of individual liberty would certainly not have permitted procedure to be overlooked. The answer to this problem is best alluded to by Miss Samuel in two passages she cited from *Areopagitica*:

> But that Plato meant this law peculiarly to that commonwealth which he imagined, and to no other, is evident. Why was he not else a lawgiver to himself but a transgressor, and to be expelled by his own magistrates; both for the wanton epigrams and dialogues which he made, and his perpetual reading of Sophron, Mimus and Aristophanes, books of grossest infamy.[14]

Although Milton recognized the spirit of Plato's political writings, he did not let him off the hook for espousing an esoteric doctrine. As Miss Samuel concluded, the student of Plato as an intelligent reader gains from the ideal states he proposed not an impossible set of legal prohibitions but a way of regarding human life and testing the worth of human aims.

As she also noted, these unwritten and unconstraining laws present a problem. Milton was here only considering the spirit in which he felt Plato laid down these rules for Crete. The "bonds and pillars" become hindrances rather than supports if enacted by statute. Milton's distrust of institutions shows itself here. To him, the man possessing virtuous knowledge would have no need for such a set of impossible procedural rules, or any confining rules for that matter. If education was to be the *fait accompli* of the commonwealth, the commonwealth will naturally possess some of its basic characteristics. In one sense, the characteristic it inherited in Milton's scheme was the lack of institutional restraint. The only mention at all of an institution in *Of Education* was the academy, which was only briefly discussed. The same was true of his commonwealth. Only the minimal institutional restraints are found. This illustrates Milton's lack as a political theorist in general. Through his minimization of any sort of necessary compulsion, his grasp of contemporary politics and of his present became quite estranged from his conception of poetry and history. By basing all of the facets of his social philosophy upon the aesthetic appreciation of poetry and virtue, he displayed a severe lack of reality pertaining to human affairs and behaviour. His concepts of historical reality and politics became as elusive as Plato's spirit. However, to Milton the didactic value of the *Laws* was in its spirit and he incorporated this into his educational scheme.

After the attainment of *proairesis* Milton's tract adopts an Aristotelian method of introducing further studies. After the reading of certain moral works his novices were to begin the study of economics and certain comedies and tragedies that dealt specifically with this subject. By economics it may be assumed that Milton meant the art of ménage, or household management. After this branch had been mastered the study of politics was introduced. This ordering of studies follows the sequence put forth by Aristotle. Book I of the *Politics* began with the theory of household management followed by the study of politics in greater detail. This is the type of ordering that leads to Milton's in-depth study of the state in the *Commonwealth*.

After these crucial studies had been mastered, and only then, did the disciplines which required the proper knowledge of good and evil present themselves—theology, church history, histories in general, heroic poetry, and tragedy. Milton felt strongly enough about the literary disciplines he included to suggest that some of their content be put to memory. These disciplines were undoubtedly singled out to be presented after the acquisition of *proairesis* because of their representation of good and (especially) evil. To the soul well fortified with virtue they could be read in their proper light rather than having their portrayal of evil bring out the worst in men's souls.

The portion of the tractate devoted to studies was divided into two sections, preceding and following *proairesis*. At the end of both sections poetry appeared as the last discipline to be studied. Before moral choice, "those poets which are now counted most hard will be both facile and pleasant: Orpheus, Hesiod . . . (etc.)." After *proairesis* the same followed the study of logic: "To which poetry would be made subsequent, or indeed, rather precedent, as being less subtle and fine . . . and show them what religious, what glorious and magnificent use might be made of poetry, both in divine and human things." Milton entered into the age-old quarrel between poetry and politics on the side of poetry. Poetry could have a didactic value in the affairs of state as it did in the relationship between Hiero and Simonides in Xenophon's dialogue. As Simonides stated to the tyrant:

> But I tell you Hiero, that the contest is against others who rule cities; if you make the city you rule the happiest of these, know well that you are victorious in the most noble and magnificent contest among human beings. First, you would at once secure the love of your subjects, which is the very thing you happen to desire. Further, not one man would herald your victory, but all human beings would sing of your virtue.[15]

Milton rejected Plato's dictum in the *Laws* concerning the threat that poets could pose to the state. Since Milton maintained the Aristotelian position that poetry expressed the universal while history expressed the particular, the subject matter of poetry will not find itself limited. Neither will it be limited to a certain type of audience, as was history. Poetry exemplified the final product of a virtuous education; history was only a tool of this process. The knowledge of which poetry was expressive (universal) was the ultimate product of a good education. History, as the expression of particular characteristics, was only a subordinate part of such an end due to its content. Miss Samuel perhaps best summed up this by citing the following passage from *An Apology* which was highly reminiscent of a similar passage in the letter to deBrass:

> And long it was not after, when I was confirmed in this opinion, that he who would frustrate of his hope to write well hereafter in laudable things, ought himself to be a true poem, that is, a composition and pattern of the best and honorablest things, not presuming to sing high praises unless he have in himself the experience and practice of all which is praiseworthy.[16]

As Miss Samuel concluded: "To be a true poet a man must live the good life."[17] To which can be added: To be a good historian a man must lead the good life.

One further point requires attention here in relation to Milton's thoughts concerning poetry and history. If poetry through education was to serve the exaltation of man's dignity on earth as well as God's in heaven, then of what specific use could it have been to the orator or statesmen? Why have honor and attention "waiting on their lips" when they spoke in public? The statesman spoke to his audience as the historian did to his; in short he was setting an example to them through his own pedagological actions. This provides an answer as to why the speaker would need an universal type of knowledge. He needed it for recognition, through which arose the ability to lead nobly. But recognition had to depend upon a proficiency in things in some way universal since it was based upon the ability to synthesize disparate elements in society.

III

The exercise of these studies continued Milton's affinity for the balanced individual. The curriculum was drawn from Milton's readings of the ancient academies of Pythagoras, Plato, Isocrates, and Aristotle. "But herein it shall exceed them and supply a defect as great as that which Plato noted in the commonwealth of Sparta." Rather than merely training youth for the occupation of war as the Spartans did, Milton proposed to make them versatile both in the arts of peace and war. Like Aristotle, Milton felt that the balance could be struck through the practice of physical exercise and music.[18]

Music, like the drama, had a "great power over dispositions and manners to smooth and make them gentle from rustic harshness and distempered passions." Its functions were to "profit and delight" and it was also supposed to aid in digestion. Milton borrowed its emotional use from the *Politics*, illustrating its similarity to the catharsis produced by tragedy. In the course of a day's studies it was necessary to indulge pupils in physical exercise. Music was to follow in order to soothe these violent passions and return their minds to scholarly pursuits. Whereas Aristotle and Plato raised objections to certain types of music and instruments because of their effect on the listener, Milton was satisfied to give this topic nothing more than cursory treatment. He would have agreed with Aristotle concerning the three possible effects of music; education, release of emotion, and benefit of cultivation, but was more interested in the second of these than the other two.

This discussion of music necessarily reverts to a problem mentioned earlier, that of compulsion. Milton's psychology was very simple but it still recognized the power of certain elements over the mind. His use of medical terminology and concepts in his drama and prose is quite interesting considering that, unlike a Marsilius, Milton had no medical training. The use of such ideas as homeopathic purgation (in *Samson Agonistes*) and catharsis in general illustrated his cognizance of the power that emotion could hold over the mind. It was undoubtedly for this reason that he shifted from Platonic to Aristotelian devices in the latter portion of the tractate. Milton did feel that some form of compulsion should be present in the education of younger children. But it was to be introduced through a controlled environment such as the self-contained academy rather than through legislation. The explicit statutes of Plato were rejected in favour of the implicit ordinances of Aristotle. Milton agreed with both writers over the effects of mimicry but rejected Plato's laws in favor of Aristotle's position:

The seeing of mimes or comedies should be forbidden to young persons by the legislator, until they have reached the age when they are allowed to share with the older men in the right of reclining and taking wine at the common tables. By that time their education will have made them immune from the evil effects of such performances.[19]

Since his own music education, as well as the observation of comedies and tragedies, followed the attainment of *proairesis*, there was no need for the statutory compulsion of Plato. *Areopagitica* provides the conclusion to this problem:

> For if they fell upon one kind of strictness, unless their care were equal to regulate all things of like aptness to corrupt the mind, that single endeavor they knew would be but a fond labor; to shut and fortify one's gate against corruption, and be necessitated to leave others round about wide open. If we think to regulate printing, thereby to rectify manners, we must regulate all recreations and pasttimes, all that is delightful to man. No music must be heard, no song set or sung, but what is grave and Doric. There must be licensing dancers, that no gesture, motion, or deportment be taught our youth but what by their allowance shall be thought honest; for such Plato was provided of.[20]

Those who were not yet capable of reason were the most susceptible to evil and must be constrained in some way. Before attaining choice it was not possible to know good by evil without the imminent possibility of succumbing to the latter. Aristotle's dictum that participation in an activity precedes judgement of the same was exactly Milton's rule concerning education. Young men incapable of choosing the right way must be instructed through a careful plan protecting them from the base. But legal prohibitions were not necessary in this respect, due to their age.

Travel abroad was purposely left for the last part of the exercise of their studies. Milton's national bias again showed itself here: "Nor shall we need the monsieurs of Paris to take our hopeful youth into their slight and prodigal custodies and send them over back transformed into mimics, apes and kickshaws." Milton's Englishman was a teacher, not a student, of his continental contemporaries: "And perhaps other nations will be glad to visit us for their own breeding or else to imitate us in their own country."

There remains little to be said concerning that last phase of education, the diet. It constituted a very small part of the tract considering it was supposed to be one of its major divisions. But since it was used as a synonym for prudence it was properly left for last. Besides being analogous to learning in that it was to be free of external diversions, it was also tacitly more than food. From *Areopagitica*:

> I conceive, therefore, that when God did enlarge the universal diet of man's body, saving over rule of temperance, he then also, as before, left arbitrary, the dieting and repasting of our minds; as wherein every mature man might have exercise his own capacity.[21]

Diet appears to have been the prudence one would have used in the intake and use of knowledge as well as food; that rigor which is undertaken after the formal supervision of the mind has terminated (after twenty-one years). It would have begun in that period of a man's life when he went abroad to enlarge his experience.

As seen earlier, the education of early youth was purposely omitted from the tractate: "... not beginning, as some have done, from the cradle, which yet might be worth many considerations."[22] Equally omitted was the role of the teacher, whose position was probably supposed to have been understood. The quality of the instructor was implied through the curriculum and amplified through it. It would be a curious note to discover how many of Milton's contemporaries were capable of teaching such a curriculum besides Milton himself:

> Only I believe this is not a bow for every man to shoot in that counts himself a teacher, but will require the sinews almost equal to those which Homer gave Ulysses . . .[23]

These mental sinews were possessed by no one other than Milton himself. As Tillyard pointed out, Milton's reasoning displayed a peculiar characteristic which bears this out. It was an inductive method which moved from the personal to the general. Thus, his educational plans were based upon his own readings and expanded into an academy and a national program. When Hartlib asked Milton for his ideas on education, he received an implicit rebuke along with it. This would only seem natural given Milton's temperament and academic background. After taking Hartlib on a peripatetic journey up the "laborious ascent" to show him the proper view of education, he presented him with the path "so smooth, so green, so full of goodly prospect." Hartlib wrote to Milton asking him for his thoughts on education and received in return, not only a letter, but a lesson.

IV

Milton's educational theory cannot be said to imply a *tabula rasa* approach to the mind even though his thought did place great emphasis upon the individual. Due to the inherent sin of Adam education became more of a remedial exercise in virtue than an end in itself. Without it man, by his fallen nature, would naturally choose evil rather than good due to the amount of pleasure involved in things of the world. The yoke of ignorance could be total. Without right reason, man was lost; he would never be able to achieve his true end either on earth or in the after-life. Reason was the sole vehicle to happiness and salvation. The direct hand of providence was as absent as the direct forces of the personification of evil. Milton usually appeared sanguine at the close of a tract such as *Of Education*. By setting reason aright he had conquered the force of evil in whatever form it appeared; the monarchy, prelacy, Catholicism, or the devil.

Milton had no conception of any modern ideas such as home environment, progressive education, etc. However, elements of such things do appear in some of his more innovative ideas. But Milton did not presage any educational innovations or even allow himself the luxury of such ideas, since the idea of reform was of primary importance. And since his idea of reform was a reversion to the classical schemes, there was no conception of the differential roles a student might have assumed in relation to his own educational experience. They were supplied with a controlled and tightly oriented environment. Unlike a Montessori approach, Milton left them little latitude within it. Their time was to be well occupied from morning until night with its vigorous program.

In conclusion of this discussion one problem in Milton's thought previously mentioned remains to be examined. Nowhere more than in *Of Education* did he allude to the rule of merit, the rule which will be explicitly mentioned in the *Commonwealth*. Political participation in Milton's sense was founded upon this particular type of rule.

Milton wrote this tract for a significant class of men; the same class that formed his primary audience and who also ruled. The reason for this lies in his conception of balance with the regime. This illustrated Milton's penchant for a classical republican form of government, of which the *Commonwealth* was merely a copy. Balance had to be struck in the commonwealth to prevent the elements of evil from gaining hegemony and by doing so, enslaving the ruled in a "conscientious slavery." An educated aristocracy of merit was Milton's solution to this possible and real hazard. Only then could Truth and Justice

Education 69

prevail. But learning took on added significance in that it contributed to the continuing process of acquisite wisdom, a form of regeneration in itself. The prevention of tyranny and the preservation of inward liberty was always easier to postpone until a later date when the products of the educational process were old enough to participate in government, thereby implying that the idealist youth had no one to blame except themselves if their concepts never bore fruition. This was the spirit of the process of acquisite wisdom.

NOTES

1. *Works* III, p. 378.
2. E.M.W. Tillyard, *Milton* (New York, 1966), p. 183. This author attributed authors outside the Bible a minor influence upon Milton's beliefs.
3. John Amos Comenius, *A Reformation of Schooles* (London, 1642) p. 42.
4. *Ibid.*, p. 43.
5. Cited in Charles Webster (ed.) *Samuel Hartlib and the Advancement of Learning* (Cambridge, 1970), p. 43.
6. John Dury, *The Reformed School* (London, n.d.), p. 3.
7. VII, 536; also the same in the *Laws*, 819 b.
8. The use to which Milton employed language and especially Latin as well as Italian pronunciation are examined by J.H. Neumann in "Milton's Prose Vocabulary," *PMLA*,LX (1945), 102 ff Neumann felt that Milton held that a lack of respect for the native tongue betokened a moral degeneration which could only end in slavery (p. 103). For this reason he advocated a thorough grounding in classical languages to avoid debasing the mother tongue.
9. Plato, *Laws*, 645 b, trans. B. Jowett (Oxford, 1968). See also C.R. Geissr, "Milton's 'Labourious Ascent'", $N + Q$, vol. 21, no. 3, March 1974, p. 94.
10. *Hughes*, p. 633.
11. *Laws*, 895 d.
12. *Hughes*, p. 733; also *PL* III 108, 117 and 129.
13. *Ibid.*, pp. 732 ff.
14. Irene Samuel, *Plato and Milton* (Ithaca, 1947), p. 60.
15. Xenophon, *Hiero or Tyrannicus*, trans. M. Kendrick, in Leo Strauss, *On Tyranny* (Ithaca, 1968), p. 19.
16. *Works* III, p. 303.
17. Samuel, p. 67.
18. J.H. Hanford cites Milton's various allusions to war and weapon training in *Of Education* as characteristic of the general humanistic education of his period, see "Milton and the Art of War," *SP* XVIII (1921), 232 ff.
19. *Politics*, 1336b 11.

20. *Hughes*, p. 732.
21. *Ibid.*, p. 727.
22. *Ibid.*, p. 639.
23. *Ibid.*

5 Liberty and the Commonwealth

Milton's proposed commonwealth was the apogee of his political and social principles. All of the various elements that comprise his social philosophy reach their logical culmination in this seemingly diverse collection of political precepts. But at the same time the *Ready and Easy Way to Establish a Free Commonwealth* was an importunate document written primarily to counter the growing trend towards a return to the Stuart monarchy. This return would have violated all of Milton's political as well as religious principles. The precepts contained in the *Commonwealth* display an urgency greater than that evidenced in *Of Education*. The attempt at instituting social and constitutional security in the state was a very real problem which demanded immediate action; more so than the concerns of a dedicated educationalist. But even though the tract was written in haste without the leisure usually attached to such treatises its importance cannot be denigrated. While its reader may wish for a more systematic approach to the subject, the *Commonwealth* was still the most succinct expression of political principles that Milton produced.

The tract was originally written after Monk's address to the Rump in March of 1660. A second edition appeared later in May of the same year. The augmented second edition will be the focus of attention here.

All of the causes of political association cease to possess their individual qualities and acquiesce to the final cause of Milton's idea of the ideal political society, the Christian commonwealth. Individual liberty could not be understood in a real political sense unless it had an environment in which to function and apply itself. The purpose of writing an heuristic history would have been useless unless it had a higher ideal to which it could administer. Acquisite wisdom was useless without a final cause through which it could manifest itself. As Milton stated in the *Art of Logic*, the end cause is that cause for which all other causes exist. They do not possess an intelligible character of their own without a final cause.

Throughout the course of this essay it has been maintained that Milton was not a man of the whole people. Regardless of this one-sided approach employed, the concept of the whole people was never totally alien from his mind. His commonwealth was the best example of this. Its primary function as a political organization was to protect the inherent inward liberty of the individual. While political community arose out of necessity its specific form of government was rather a matter of convention. The true subjective religious nature of such an organization was quite evident:

> And what government comes nearer to this precept of Christ than a free commonwealth, wherein they who are greatest, are perpetual servants and drudges to the public at their own cost and charges.[1]

The examination of the *Commonwealth* must begin in a typically Miltonic fashion, from the top down. Terms such as authority, sovereignty, and power all have their peculiar aspects in Milton's language which were not employed in a strict systematic sense.

I

Although the *Commonwealth* attempted to come to grips with a political body composed of all men, the penchant for the ablest was nonetheless evident:

> The other part of our freedom (besides inward liberty) consists in the civil rights and advancements of every person according to his merit: the enjoyment of those never more certain, and the access to those never more open, than in a free commonwealth.[2]

Even if understood in an egalitarian context of the idea of inward liberty as being common to all men, this was not a democratic statement. Civil rights were not a matter of natality to Milton; the only equality that he was willing to concede by birth was that of an intrinsic freedom according to nature. A vast gulf divided man in an individual state of nature in contrast to man as a member of the body politic:

> And what the people but a herd confus'd
> A miscellaneous rabble, who extol
> Things vulgar, and well-weighed, scarce worth the praise?
> They praise and they admire, they know not what;
> And know not whom, but as one leads the other[3]

Liberty and the Commonwealth 73

It is at the basis of political association that a major problem in Milton's political thought is encountered. If political equality can be imputed to Milton at all, it arises from statements such as the following from the *Tenure of Kings and Magistrates*:

> No man who knows aught can be so stupid to deny that all men were naturally born free, being the image of and resemblance of God himself, and were, by privilege above all the creatures born to command, and not to obey.[4]

But political rights were not a corollary of this condition. Human destiny was substantially altered by the loss of grace and right reason:

> ... and they lived so, till from the root of Adam's transgression falling among themselves to do wrong and violence, and foreseeing that such courses must needs tend to the destruction of all, they agreed by common league to bind each other from mutual injury, and jointly to defend themselves against any that gave disturbance to such agreement.[5]

The equality of man was predicated upon the conception that freedom could not be impugned. It could be preserved in civil society regardless of the damage done by the Fall. Milton adopted an anti-Augustinian position in this matter. Rather than espousing the strict theological position that saw man's nature after the Fall as substantially different from the prelapsarian state, Milton held to the immutability doctrine of man's essence.[6] Although sin and mortality had been placed upon mankind as a result of the first sin, the original options of choice were still left open. There was no doubt, however, that the right choice would be harder to make considering the given circumstances. But as seen earlier, Milton adhered to the seminal identity theory of Augustine. This complicates his thought considerably. This pessimistic view of man's behaviour and generation appears to be diametrically opposed to the sanguine philosophic conception of his unalterable potential. By advocating that man's nature and goodness were intrinsically implanted by God and that this state could not change, his thought strongly resembled that of Pelagius.[7] But by adhering to the seminal identity concept he broke with that position and added an Augustinian element which was to permeate his thought and add a curious tension to the institutions of his commonwealth. While not denying the generative elements of the innate ability to sin:

... man was made in the image of God, and had the whole law of nature so implanted and innate within him, that he needed no precept to enforce its observance, it follows, that if he received any additional commands, whether respecting the tree of knowledge or the institution of marriage, these commands formed no part of the law of nature, which is sufficient of itself to teach whatever is agreeable to right reason, that is to say, whatever is intrinsically good. Such commands therefore must have been founded upon what is called positive right, whereby God, or any one invested with lawful power, commands what is in itself neither good nor bad, and what therefore would not have been obligatory on anyone, had there been no law to enjoin or prohibit it.[8]

Political power, which based its authority upon law, was a product of the Fall. This was made clear in *Paradise Lost*:

Since thy original lapse, true liberty
Is lost, which always with right Reason dwells
Twinn'd, and from her hath no individual being:
Reason in man obscur'd, or not obeyed,
Immediately inordinate desires
And upstart Passions catch the Government
From Reason, and to servitude reduce
Man till then free.[9]

Coercion took the place of reason in government. Specifically, in the language of Milton's logic, political power was achieved by this coercion:

Something is done by coercion when the efficient cause is driven to the effect, as when a stone is thrown upward or horizontally which by its nature is borne downward. This is called the necessity of coercion and is able sometimes to happen even to free causes.[10]

The force of original sin on man's soul acted as an external principle to the internal ones of nature and reason. Originally, pre-lapsarian association was structured by the intrinsic freedom in nature. This situation was not changed by the loss of grace. But the diversion of reason was coercion by an external agent. As in the analogy of the stone tossed upward, society could return to its pristine state of grace abounding where equality and freedom would prevail. But to do so, coercion (in this case political power) would have to be overcome or rectified. The agent was to be the dominance of the internal principles of the soul, namely reason and the will.

It may be asked whether this can be considered an effect of cause through accident since man brought the Fall upon himself. But rather than saying that positive right cannot alter man's nature, the necessary political corollary must be added that neither can man himself do or have done so. Thus, the force which acted upon the state of grace and polluted it with wrong reason was not an element of the human condition until that time and therefore must be considered strictly as an alien force.

In this way, the freedom that originated in the state of nature became the convenient method Milton employed to control the coercive political power. Through a correct application of this freedom or natural equality, sovereignty resided in the people; it was their possession to do with as they chose. This was the argument employed in the vindication of the execution of Charles I. But the unbridled masses themselves became shackled. Although political power resided in the people as a whole, political authority did not. The latter was a derivative power only. This was a reassertion of Milton's bias about who knew what was best for whom. Advocates of a mixed regime had often before made this assumption that the delegation of authority in the regime could not reside in any one particular estate but should be somewhat evenly distributed to the three principle estates in classical republican thought, where this concept originated. Political power and the state were synonymous terms in his language. Both were extraneous forces to the true efficients of Christian society, faith and charity.

Proceeding from this postulate, the problem arises not in where true power lay or in its delegation but in the true nature of the coercive power in the state. Political power was man's possession, political authority his servant. Authority was delegated only and to be administered by those who could administer it best. This was the crux of Milton's idea of political participation. His concept of justice was quite elementary; it simply stated that every men should get his due. In the language of Aristotle and Hobbes, the application of this was known as distributive justice. But in order to keep justice on a Christian plane, Milton based it upon the ability to be regenerate. Proceeding from this, if one's due was greater than that of others based upon his positive contribution to society, recognition was due him. And this type of person naturally ruled because the regenerate (and necessarily élite) group which he represented had a greater sense of basic equity and its derivative distributive type of justice. The coercive power had a Platonic-Christian paradigm and thus the idea of justice enacted through charity legitimatized it through the usual Miltonic sense of social progress and regeneration.

II

The enigma presented by a first glance at the distribution of authority in the commonwealth follows naturally from this position. But before an examination of this can be initiated, the Christian nature of the proposed regime must be explicated in general terms. This is necessary for two reasons. First, a valid idea of the Christian commonwealth must be established before its intricacies can be examined. Secondly, it must be established that Milton was not an advocate of civil disobedience and that his adherence to inward liberty to the extreme was in logical accordance with his preliminary suppositions.

Civil power was an object of distrust to Milton. His *Treatise of Civil Power in Ecclesiastical Causes* was an argument centered around what the state could not do. Its basic argument proceeded syllogistically from the major premise that all coercive power was evil. In this treatise individual liberty was equated with the religious for political purposes. Individual liberty was simply beyond the jurisdiction of civil power. This was obvious to Milton for two reasons. It was both anterior to it in point of time and spiritually closer to God, being his direct link with man. Even church government did not possess the ability to dictate to the individual interpreter of his own faith, and,

> ... if church government cannot use force in religion ... because they cannot infallibly determine to the conscience without convincement, much less have civil magistrates authority to use force where they can much less judge.[11]

Coercive external power was force without authority and needed a legitimizing factor. Ostensibly, it would appear that the ready answer was the rule of law. This this was not the case. Humanity had been burdened with coercive power since the Fall and in the case of Britain particularly, this power had yet to be rectified. Since the basic relationship in society was that of one to his neighbor, the answer lies within this context. The benevolent charity which characterized this fundamental relationship was to be extended to the political realm. Through this approach, reason, which dictated charity to the conscience and will, would re-emerge in a lawful authoritative context. Justice would again be reinstated to all elements in society. The concept of giving each citizen his due was to be achieved through the rule of charity and reason in a meritocracy.

Milton conceived of the political bond as a moral covenant with judicial considerations playing a secondary role:

> No understanding man can be ignorant that covenants are ever made according to the present state of persons and of things, and have ever the general laws of nature and of reason included in them though not expressed. If I make a voluntary covenant as with a man to do him good and afterward he prove a monster to me, I should conceive a disobligement . . . nor know I covenant so sacred that witholds me from demanding justice on him.[12]

The moral nature of covenants was bound to the state of nature and natural right was preserved in society by conceiving of this bond as ethical rather than merely legal. The government could not be separated from the body politic any more than form could be divorced from matter. The state was only as healthy as its rulers. When one became perverted it only reflected the malaise of the other. And since authority was only delegated and never transferred, abuse of such authority led to the dissolution of the bond: "who therefore kills a king must kill him while he is king."[13]

The moral basis for the vindication of regicide rested upon the Greek definition of the perversion of monarchy. Milton never denied that kingship was one of the three best forms of government in the classical sense but he did emphasize that its perversion into tyranny was the worst. He also conceived of monarchy in a larger pluralistic society than that of the Greek *polis* as somewhat anachronistic. Once Britain had thrown off the yoke of monarchy there was to be no return. This was not based upon philosophic conjecture or subscription to a Polybian type theory of government but merely a matter of practicality and security:

> But admit that monarchy of itself may be convenient to some nations, yet to us who have thrown it out, received back again, it cannot but prove pernicious. For kings to come, never forgetting their former ejection, will be sure to fortify themselves sufficiently for the future against all such attempts hereafter from the people.[14]

The executive function vested in one person was thus discarded. To find a suitable replacement Milton turned to the "middle way" expounded in the theories of Aristotle, Cicero, and Polybius—the oligarchic element fused with the popular.

III

Milton's advocacy of a perpetual council or senate has been an issue of considerable consternation among historians and political theorists who have understood it as the ultimate sell-out by a putative libertarian thinker. "Can one read it," asked John Adams, "without shuddering?"[15] Through his explosive rhetoric and incisive political sallies Milton appeared at times to waver in his political principles. But when he advocated a perpetual council on a grand scale he did no more than reach the conclusion of a political system pervaded by élitism and a strong concept of noblesse oblige. The council did not theoretically diminish liberty in the commonwealth but did in fact give the best illustration of what is called "classical republicanism."

The grand council was to be chosen from the ablest of the nation for the common good. Sovereignty was to be delegated to it; the residual power which originated in the public sector was not to be transferred. The council was to possess all powers and functions necessary to the national interest, e.g. maintenance of national armed forces, management of the public revenue, power of treaty concerning commerce and foreign relations, and proposal of civil laws. For affairs of extreme urgency or national security a council of state elected from the general council was proposed. In contrast to general parliamentary practice, the council was emphatically not meant to be successive, or in Milton's language, non-standing or non-perpetual. No period of general election or politicking was to break the continuity of this body in any way.

Milton wavered momentarily in the second edition of the *Commonwealth* with respect to this perpetuity:

> ... if it be feared that the long continuance of power may corrupt sincerest men, the known expedient is, and by some lately propounded, that annually (or if the space be longer, so much perhaps the better) the third part of senators may go out according to the precedence of their election, and the like number be chosen in their places, to prevent the settling of too absolute a power, if it should be perpetual—and this they call partial rotation.[16]

The reference here was to Harrington's proposal in *Oceana* which suggested that each shire in Britain contribute to a senate of three hundred knights and an assembly of one thousand fifty deputies, each being contingent upon a triennial rotation or an annual change of one third its membership. But Milton saw this as leaving too much to chance. He went on in the next paragraph to conclude:

> But I wish that this wheel or partial wheel in state, if it be possible, might be avoided, as having too much affinity with the wheel of Fortune.

This particular statement must be understood in the context of the urgency with which Milton undertook his project as well as his particular desire to provide his model with internal security. Aristotle had noted that regardless of the amount of planning man does, events are still left a great deal to chance. But Milton refused to loosen his grip upon the proposed regime. Rather than acknowledging fortune, or even determinism, he sought to keep a tight control over the selection of senators. Thus, when Aristotle spoke of accident and chance as "causes of the goods external to the soul" and continued that no "man can be just and temperate merely by accident or simply through chance,"[17] he provided the principle Milton adopted in the *Commonwealth*. Since the regime was to provide for the common happiness of all its citizenry (and happiness was a good of the soul as Aristotle maintained) then nothing which affected such a good could be left to the caprice of fortune. An "external good", or chance, would have nothing to do with Milton's proposal for the "internal good" of his commonwealth; that is, happiness achieved through the rule of the ablest.

The concept of legitimate authority within the state as an internal good, or good of the soul, was also proposed by Harrington in his *Oceana*. Distinguishing between power and authority as external and internal goods based upon reason and passion respectively, he classified authority as the true element of reason in the state. The body politic, being likened to an organic whole or soul, must be ruled by an internal rational principle compatible with itself. Milton employed this general idea with a Christian twist which cast a dubious light upon the rule of law in society.

The employment of such a concept synthesized with the Christian ethical overtones plus the supposition that merit was the only way to achieve a harmonious state were the legitimizing factors behind the advocacy of the perpetual senate. On this basis Milton could also reject the traditional remedy devised to counter or balance a senate:

> It will be objected that in most places where they had perpetual senates, they had also popular remedies against their growing too imperious . . . But the event tells us that those remedies either little availed the people, or brought them to such licentious and unbridled democracy as in fine ruined themselves with their own excessive power . . . so that the main reason urged why popular assemblies are to be trusted with the people's liberty, rather than a senate of principal men . . . is by experience found false.[18]

This position was not arrived at through philosophic enquiry any more than his ideas concerning a return to monarchy were but rather through Milton's own empirical historical findings. He waved a theoretical, systematic approach to the deterioration of government and instead adhered to the idea that monarchy will degenerate directly into mob rule if left unchecked.

The council was to be chosen through a refining process by which the qualified would select out of their own number the ablest and submit their names to nomination: "out of that number . . . to choose a less number more judiciously, till after a third or fourth sifting and refining of exactest choice they only be left chosen who are the due number and seem by most voices the worthiest."[19] In order to enable the populace to do so, educational reform would be necessary.

This process provided the commonwealth with the first of two unique institutions. As Milton stated: "the balance therefore must be exactly so set as to preserve and keep due authority on either side, as well in the Senate as in the people." The deliberative element in the state was purposely placed in the hands of the few. Aristotle classified this in the *Politics* as the power of oligarchy in that some citizens were in effect deliberating for all. Other than the original refining process, the public at large had no power of deliberation in Milton's scheme. The function of the council would be oligarchic but in light of a common good the few would in fact be ruling for all rather than for themselves alone. In this manner, the political function shifts from that of an oligarchy to that of an aristocracy, or the rule of merit. As Aristotle classified it, a polity was a combination of oligarchy and democracy; when it inclined toward oligarchy it was called an aristocracy. Polybius best described the balance at which Milton aimed: "Nor again can we style every oligarchy an aristocracy, but only that where the government is in the hands of a selected body of the justest and wisest men."[20]

The question remains here of how this commonwealth was to be balanced. The first of the three elements in the Aristotelian definition of a constitution, the deliberative, was instituted in favor of the few. This was also true to an extent of the second element—the magisterial. Whereas the deliberative function encompassed the general affairs of state, the magisterial was more specific. It had to do with the administration of these powers. Now this power resided in the Senate but was also evident in the local form of government Milton proposed. Civil rights could be best proposed if,

> ... every county in the land were made a kind of subordinate commonality or commonwealth ... where the nobility and chief gentry from a proportionate compass of territory annexed to each city may build houses or palaces befitting their quality, may bear part in the government, make their own judicial laws.[21]

It was from this element of society on the local level that new members to the perpetual council could be chosen if vacancies occurred.

Through the local form of government he advocated, Milton gave a clear definition of what he meant by the "people." There appears to be no trace of a democratic idea of the franchise for all or even of letting all of the people participate in some form of political activity. This was rather to be performed for them by the local "nobility." With the disdain Milton displayed for the king's former court and his advocacy of the abolition of the Lords, it was obvious that nobility in this case did not mean hereditary or regally-conferred title but rather nobility of virtue. In this last above-quoted passage is one of the only places that Milton even alluded to a property qualification of any sort in his political writings. The "people" were only those who had achieved a decent station in life, either by merit or possibly birth. There is enough mention of the misguided or abused "multitude" in the *Commonwealth* and the other political tracts to suspect that it excluded all those who were not literate to a fair degree.

The power of the Senate was ubiquitous in the *Commonwealth* since even the local forms of government resembled it in an oligarchic or aristocratic fashion. In this case a property qualification of some sort was added. But neither form provided the constitutional check upon the other to prevent authority from going awry. If this was to be a truly mixed regime as Milton intended, it was not to be understood as one in the juristic sense. One additional power resided in the Senate which eradicated any doubt about the nature of authority in this polity. Z.S. Fink pointed out that the term dictator, or one who held this type of power, maintained a different political position in the seventeenth century than the one normally associated with it today. A person granted the dictatorial power in Milton's day was usually provided with it constitutionally in times of stress or national emergency and was accountable for that power, or not, as so specified.[22] This was exactly the case with the Senate in the *Commonwealth*. The urgency with which the tract was written and the easier accessibility to the council provided for at the end of the pamphlet after security had been established both testify to this. Milton granted a dictatorial power to his grand council; overtly so in the council of state. While Milton did not invest this power in one person he obviously did so with regard to the Senate. Milton had too much distrust of civil power to enable it to run amuck in times of shaky internal security. However, when the institutions became stabilized and the educative process had taken a firm position, then the dictatorial power could loosen its hold. This was obviously a different tone from the importunate beginning of the tract. It also leads to the other factor of this regime which now must be examined, the local form of government.

The third Aristotelian element of government, the judicial, rested with the people on the local level. However, this included only the administration of law and not its initiation:

> So they shall have justice in their own hands, law executed fully and finally in their own counties and precincts, long wished and spoken of, but never yet obtained. They shall have none to blame but themselves if it not be well administered, and fewer laws to expect from the supreme authority.[23]

Milton also used terms such as *vote* in his treatises and never fully explained what he meant by them. This is a general problem with his unsystematic procedure. But the judicatory power was placed in the hands of the populace specifically. Following the spirit of Harrington's aphorism that "arbitrary power, going upon the interest of one or a few, makes not a just judicatory,"[24] Milton was careful to place it in the hands of what he considered the many; the local element. But as a modern reader would see it, this was nevertheless highly oligarchic. As Aristotle maintained, "the sort of (judicatory power) in which membership is drawn from a section, and the courts decide on all matters, is oligarchical."[25]

The model did not provide any institutional or constitutional means for the redress of grievances to the grand council. The only modicum of this tacitly mentioned was the publication of assenting or dissenting opinions by the local authorities which were to be sent to the Senate. In his letter to Monk Milton did mention this, but again not as much as could be hoped for. The grand council possessed its general powers,

> ... but not without assent of the standing council in each city, or such other general assembly as may be called on such occasion, from the whole territory where they may without much trouble deliberate on all things fully, and send their suffrages up within a short time, by deputies appointed.

In such a manner, i.e. by borrowing from the chief classical models of a mixed regime, Milton devised his own version of the free mixed commonwealth.

IV

Two questions remained unanswered in Milton's political system. The first is the exact nature of the citizen and the second is the precise position of law in society. It appears, if representation in his commonwealth can be considered in a linear manner with the Senate at the apex and the people at the other end of the line, that Milton effectively severed the masses from political participation by destroying the mobile vertical structure which would have served political movement. This was done between two specific points; those occupied by the places of the local assemblies and the national Senate. Between those points mobility was indeed difficult if not functionally impossible, at least until the commonwealth had achieved some sort of internal order. The concept of citizen originated at the apex of this line and changed into a diluted, mutated form as it descended.

The nature of the citizen has at various times been alluded to in this essay as the product of an élite educative process, the virtuous or morally noble, or he who had contributed the most to the positive common happiness. The interrelationship of these concepts in the context that has been considered here points back to the use Milton made of ontology in explicating his ideas. As originally seen in relation to *Of Education*, certain concepts can never be escaped in dealing with particular facets of his thought. As stated earlier, the educated gentleman was the pillar and sustenance of Milton's commonwealth. Except in a negative context, the more mundane issues of political reality were never fully delineated. In all of Milton's thought only piecemeal adumbrations exist of political concepts such as the whole of the body politic or the role of positive law.

This elliptical quality provides the most curious paradox of all in his thought. The law of God, which was immanent in nature, was kept intact in his social thought. But the institutional requisites of the commonwealth did not correspond to the essence of man understood either as fallen from grace or as essentially good but rather a combination of the two. The rule of virtue, which would correspond to man's immutable nature, was fused with rigid institutional control which at first glance would suggest that the author was a thoroughgoing Augustinian or perhaps even a Manichean in arguing that evil was imminent in nature along with good. But this strange commonwealth lacked the bite which would have made it a near totalitarian oligarchy. Pervading these steadfast institutions was the rule of charity. The obvious question arises here of whom Milton really distrusted. Fink came very near the answer:

> The reader will doubtless feel that Milton's discovery that the better part of the people could be taken as standing for the whole even when they were a numerical minority removed whatever genuinely popular elements there may have been in his political theory. The fact, however, that there would appear to be nothing truly democratic about Milton's conception of the people in 1660 must not be permitted to obscure the fact that he saw the better part of the people as constituting the democratic element in his ideal commonwealth.[26]

Perhaps the simplest answer as to why he could not numerically include all in his scheme was provided in two rhetorical passages. Concerning the liberty of the marriage bond and divorce and the subsequent outcry that followed the publication of these unorthodox ideas, he described his opponents as those,

> that bawl for freedom in their senseless mood,
> And still revolt when the Truth would set them free.
> License they mean when they cry liberty;
> For who loves that must first be wise and good.[27]

The same spirit was evident in the introduction to the *Tenure of Kings and Magistrates*: "For, indeed none can love freedom heartily but good men; the rest love not freedom but license, which never hath more scope or more indulgence than under tyrannts."

The original tension manifest in the immutability doctrine of man's nature vs. the seminal identity theory emerged in a political context. All men were by nature good but some (probably most) could not be trusted implicitly. Thus, institutions were proposed which, while frightening most of their later readers, were seen by the author as the paradigms of virtue and goodness. The whole potential of Adam was evident in the causes of political association; the worst degeneration and license of the human condition was protected against in its steadfast institutions.

The good man and the good citizen were the same. Milton could adhere to this only because his commonwealth was to be the ideal. Following a strict Aristotelian construction, the qualities of the citizen and the good man remained in proportion only as long as the state did not require the former to do something contrary to the latter's nature. When all existed in harmony, the relationship was ideal. This was Milton's political thought in both capsule form and in its entirety. Only the variable in this triad, the civil power, was essentially base.

V

Milton's commonwealth was the culmination of an idea which originated in the state of nature. Viewed as a whole it does not present any inconsistencies. Unlike Hobbes, Milton maintained the proposition that natural right could be preserved in society without reversion to a state of chaos. By doing so, he sought to rectify the sovereign political power rather than forcing it into a strict equation with the original covenant producing an absolute sovereign body. Like the Cambridge Platonists, he grounded his system in ethics rather than acknowledging that the political power was the absolute master. In the words of Harrington: "as the form of a man is the image of God, so the form of a government is the image of man."[28] Milton's weakness as a political thinker was due to the fact that he never successfully bridged the gap between the two images because of his *idée fixe* with seminal identity.

NOTES

1. *Hughes*, p. 885.
2. *Ibid.*, p. 896.
3. *PR* III, 49–53.
4. *Hughes*, p. 754. Also see C.R. Geisst, "Milton and Brutus: Born to Command", *N + Q*, Nov. 1974, vol. 21, p. 412/413.
5. *Ibid.*
6. W. Grace, "Milton, Salamasius, and the Natural Law," *JHI*, XXIV (1963), 324.

7. Pelagius held that man possessed an unconditional free will and was not subjected to a law of nature but rather had the ability to accomplish the divine will by his own choice. There were, then, three features of action; power, will and realization. The first came from God but the other two expressly belonged to man. By the power of action, freedom of choice was still linked to the consent of God. Pelagius differed from Augustine by holding that sin was propagated by custom and example rather than by generation. He also held that each soul was created by God; a position in antithesis to Milton's. The relation between Pelagius and Milton suffers from Pelagius' theory of the propagation of the soul and body in distinction to Milton's traducianist theory but the more immediate theory of the nature of man in general is the important link between them.
8. *Works* XV, p. 117.
9. XII, 83–90.
10. *Works* XI, p. 45.
11. *Ibid.*, p. 842.
12. *Hughes*, p. 768. This statement appears to have been a definite rejection of Hobbes' conception of the irrevocable political contract; see *Leviathan*, I, 14.
13. *Hughes*, p. 769.
14. Ibid.
15. Cited in G.P. Gooch, *English Democratic Ideas in the Seventeenth Century* (Cambridge, 1954), p. 268.
16. *Hughes*, p. 889.
17. *Politics* 1323b 10.
18. *Hughes*, p. 890.
19. *Ibid*, p. 891.
20. Polybius, *The Histories*, trans. W.R. Paton (London, 1923), VI, 4.
21. *Hughes*, p. 896.
22. Z.S. Fink, "Political Implications of Paradise Regained", *JEGP*, XL (1941), 485.
23. *Hughes*, p. 896.
24. "A System of Politics", in *Oceana and Other Works* (London, 1771), p. 479.
25. *Politics* 1301a 10.
26. Fink, *Classical Republicans*, 2nd ed. (Evanston, 1962), p. 116.
27. From *Sonnet XIII*.
28. Harrington, *Works*, p. 462.

6 Republican Thought and Historical Analysis

The absence of a descriptive effect of social causation other than a general teleological conception of the good life in Milton's scheme separated him from the chiliasts and utopian thinkers of his period. Milton did not emphasize the end of political life as much as he did the efficient. Although "the effect is by virtue of all the causes, it is named the effect from the principal cause, that is, the efficient (cause)."[1] Observing his thought in this manner also provides an invaluable aid to his reader. Since Milton's thought understood as a system has its inconsistencies, it is difficult to evaluate it on this basis. But if it is viewed through the perspective of its most important element it can be more clearly understood.

Chapter I examined all causes in the pattern except the primal cause. This was only acknowledged to be a genus of God's goodness. Only after the other causes have been described can this one be defined. The concept of the *people* is the primal cause in Milton's thought. This *people* is to be distinguished from the populace which comprised the matter of the commonwealth. The difference between the two terms is the tension that existed between man's potential and his actuality, tainted by a generative idea of sin. The latter actuality is the basis of the commonwealth, its natural component. There are, then, two subtle conceptions of the *people* at work throughout Milton's writings, which a brief recapitulation will make clear.

The concept of liberty evolved out of a theology which conceived of all matter as being created good and intrinsically free. Liberty in its incipient state was obeying the faculty which enabled creatures to pursue their natural end in accordance with this state of God-given grace, which thoroughly permeated all aspects of creation. Into this state of universal goodness man was introduced with the same natural characteristics, including a free will. This idyllic state was negated by the sin of pride and arrogance which introduced chaos into the world. As a result mankind was burdened with the punishment of death, which affected the soul as well as the body. But regardless of the death of the soul, the doctrine of the indestructability of matter suggested that mankind would someday arise to regain paradise. This process was set in motion by Christ, who expiated the sin of Adam by his own sacrificial death. But this symbolic form of atonement did not totally vitiate the destructiveness of sin upon man. Even in the regenerate state man still possessed the innate ability to sin, which was transmitted from father to son as an integral part of the human condition. This primevil development was the basis of Milton's social thought.

The political contract evolved out of this state of human imperfection. Its immediate occasion was the necessity of self-preservation. The *jus naturale* of man was to be preserved intact regardless of any compactual agreement and the civil law was to aim at a common good with this in mind. Natural right itself was the higher conception of good and justice which man was to attempt through the faculty of reason. Even though Milton's state of prehistory was markedly different from the historical, the one common factor to both was the divinely-oriented state of right; necessity could not obviate this or compromise it in civil government. The raison d'état, or more appropriately, raison d'être of society was the immediate preservation of the state of virtue which characterized man's original goodness. The institution devised to protect liberty, both positive and negative, was that one which would further permanent social ideals imbued with the Christian concepts of love and faith. The Christian commonwealth sought to achieve this through a set of rigid institutional strictures such as the perpetual senate, within which was lodged a dictatorial power, and a local form of government instituted along the same lines. Through such devices the innate ability of man to sin was to be protected against while equally allowing his potential to flourish. The best means to achieve this end was to provide a scheme of virtuous education for the youth of the nation. Then the fears of those who anticipated a ruling obligarchy in fact rather than a virtuous aristocracy would be best allayed. If all of these tenets would be followed, then the true sovereign of man—reason—would take its place as the real ruling force in government above the will.

The pattern of social causation then places its prime focus upon the efficient cause of society. It may be argued that Milton's method placed more emphasis upon the disposition of this particular argument than upon the demonstration of a logical explanation. This was true of the Ramistic method in general. But as has been pointed out all along, the potential for social justice had always existed in Milton's mind and whether or not this method of argumentation was merely emphasizing the means rather than the demonstrative argument is not of primary importance. The most important factor here was obviating the social effects of seminal identity which appeared most flagrantly in the matter of the commonwealth. Since the social consequences of generation could not be overcome entirely, the obvious focus of attention of subsequent social proposals would have to be on the potential of each man to be regenerate. Here lies the origins of inequality in Milton's thought.

I

Chapter I posited that Milton's social philosophy had a weak foundation based upon his lack of a permanent concept of human nature. In political perspective this analysis remains valid. If the prime concern here had been theological thought, on the other hand, this tension would have been of less importance. But the basic inconsistency in this scheme was still common to both realms. Simply, Milton held to two conceptions of equality; one in the general sense and one in a particular.

The omitted primal cause in the causative pattern assumed that all men were created equal (as originally propounded in the *Tenure of Kings and Magistrates*). How then are some better equipped to rule than others, or more importantly, how can an élitist republican government be posited on this basis? The problem centers around what Milton conceived of as equality. Obviously it was not a political equality but something more indigenous to all men, originally evidenced in the state of nature. This was the equality of goodness; not political rights but *jus naturale*. As creatures of God all men were created equal and were so before the Fall. After the victory of the fallen will goodness alone was not the basis of society and inequality was introduced based upon the will. Those with the stronger volition were superior to those who were weaker.

The basic political syllogism Milton employed illustrates this idea. Although the syllogism can only prove a particular conclusion in order to retain its nature, it does nevertheless illustrate Milton's ideas on the subject.

major premise: all men are created good.
minor premise: some men are politically equal.
conclusion: some men politically equal are good.[2]

The obvious fact here is that not all the politically equal are good. To accept this syllogism an agreement must certainly be reached as to whether the premises are valid. It has already been shown that the major premise is thoroughly Miltonic. The minor premise finds its best documentation in *Of Education* and the *Commonwealth* through their explicit élitism. Although it would have violated Milton's rules of logic to draw a universal conclusion from general and particular sets of premises, the particular conclusion reached here achieves the same desired effect in a negative way. Rather than proving that all men are good but some better than others this conclusion achieves the same end in argumentation. Here lies the refutation of democracy in Milton's scheme. Milton was not granting equality and simply urging an indirect form of government to facilitate matters. What he did was deny that all men retained their original equality and instituted a government which bore this out. Thus, after the Fall goodness was not sufficient to cope with the necessity of society which required a stronger will than ever to regain paradise. A perverse will fused with reason could all but wipe out man's goodness. Historically, this idea was known as the "yoke." Only a will fused with right reason would imply a state of equality for those who remained intellectually and morally attuned. But politically, the only generalization which Milton would permit stated that since all men have a natural right and since a citizen is a man, a citizen has a natural right. But what he also had was an appetitive will, which vitiated all democratic corollaries of that right.

The natural order was then one of a basic inequality in terms of the ruling principle. An aristocratic order was the natural tenor of society around which all of Milton's social thought revolved. In order to fully actualize the potential of his being, man had to constantly bring out the best of himself. The *History of Britain* in particular demonstrated Milton's cognizance of the Aristotelian notion that self-knowledge can be achieved by the study of externals.[3] The same was true of the attainment of *proairesis* in *Of Education*, where the youth of the nation could become better citizens by fulfilling the maxim "know thyself be thyself" through a rigid curriculum. Therefore, to reduce inequality to its basic factor is to revert to the state of wisdom. The difference between men is intellectual; the wiser are the better. While inequality proceeds from the will, the avenue to equality is the triumph of reason. Wisdom is that type of reason which exercises a prudent choice. This is one step above Hobbes' theory of self-preservation based upon will. While Hobbes' citizen sought protection based upon the golden rule, Milton's citizen sought it through the spirit of justice which the rule epitomized rather than through the fear of physical reprisal.

The roles of practical and theoretical wisdom are central to Milton's philosophy. The process of knowing oneself and being oneself was explicated in the *Commonwealth* as realizing two types of liberty, the spiritual and the civil.[4] To possess one was to possess the other. Spiritual liberty was that knowledge of the Almighty common to all men; the type of knowledge known as universal. Civil liberty was rather the practical knowledge needed to regain paradise. This distinction between the two forms of knowledge was verified in Raphael's reply to Adam in *Paradise Lost* concerning the knowledge of angels and men:

> Fancy and understanding, whence the Soul
> Reason receives, and reason is her being,
> Discursive, or Intuitive; discourse
> Is oftest yours, the latter most is ours,
> Differing but in degree, of kind the same.[5]

II

Milton's philosophy is unique in one historical respect that cannot be overlooked. Like the Cambridge Platonists, his thought was avowedly anti-Hobbesian. It becomes difficult to ascertain whether Milton overstated his case in some respects due to the ever-present shadow of *Leviathan*. But even a cursory analysis makes one point quite clear. In relation to Hobbes' philosophy which displayed a well-ordered system, Milton's theory was rather sketchy and concomitantly sanguine as a result.

Hobbes' secularization of the end of society is a convenient place to illustrate his marked difference with Milton:

> The final cause, end, or design of men, who naturally love liberty, and dominion over others, in which we see them live in commonwealths, is the foresight of their own preservation . . . which is not to be had from the law of nature.[6]

Since the law of nature was that of partiality and pride rather than love and equity, force held the commonwealth together and steered it on course toward its end. The tension between this and Milton is obvious. Unlike the Hobbesian position of preserving the inherent desire of self-preservation by systematically destroying any loosely interpreted ideas such as conscience and full liberty, which were inimical to society, Milton sought to extend them free reign. Hobbes provided the original position to which proponents of a free conscience retaliated:

> ... I observe the disease of a commonwealth, that proceed from the position of seditious doctrines, whereof one is, that *every private man is judge* of good and evil actions. This is true in the condition of mere nature, where there are no civil laws; and also under civil government, in such cases as are not determined by the law. But otherwise, it is manifest, that the measure of good and evil actions, is the civil law; and the judge the legislator, who is always representative of the commonwealth. From this false doctrine, men are disposed to debate with themselves and dispute the commands of the commonwealth and afterwards to obey, or disobey them, as in their private judgements they shall think fit; whereby the commonwealth is distracted and weakened.[7]

While Hobbes recognized the need for conscience, he simply subordinated it to the civil power to protect against subversion, thereby creating what is commonly called "negative" liberty. In short, Milton's conception of the civil power proceeded deductively from the position of what it could not do while Hobbes' position was just the opposite.

Hobbes' affinity for the sovereign power necessarily led him to legitimatize that power at the cost of the individual. The sovereign was an entity in itself which found its best expression in the monarchial form:

> And because he is a sovereign, he requireth obedience to all his own, that is, to all civil laws; which also are contained in the laws of nature, that is all the laws of God: for besides the laws of nature, and the laws of the Church, which are part of the civil law, (for the Church that can make laws is the commonwealth) there can be no other laws divine. Whosoever therefore obeyeth his Christian sovereign, is not thereby hindered, neither from believing, nor from obeying God.[8]

To this position Milton replied with the closest thing in his lexicon concerning power—the state of nature. This law was his omnipotent sovereign, and,

... not the common Law, nor the civil, but piety and justice, that are our foundresses; they stoop not, neither change colour for *Aristocracy*, *democracy*, or *Monarchy*, nor yet at all interrupt their just courses, but far above the taking notice of those inferior niceties with perfect sympathy, wherever they meet, kiss each other.[9]

Milton's denigration of civil law and all governmental forms save his own commonwealth is a curious problem which has no immediate answer. Thus, in the positions maintained by the two theorists are evidenced the extremes of the concept of sovereign power; all or none at all.

Hobbes' distinction of commonwealth by acquisition or institution has no parallel in Milton's thought. Since Milton conceived of a commonwealth as one "large Christian personage" maintained by justice and charity it is difficult to state conclusively whether this was a natural or acquired characteristic. The least that can be said though is that it was the most natural form of government. But Hobbes' position, maintaining that subjects could not change the form of government because of the nature of the covenant which saw each man as the author of his own deeds and subsequently of the political contract as well, was in direct opposition to Milton's pronouncements in the regicide tracts. Neither did Milton rationalize that since the subject is author of the institution's acts and that the sovereign acts for all, then the sovereign is above the civil law. But yet there is a relation here between the accessibility to sovereign power in both thinkers. Hobbes' sovereign, above the civil law, and Milton's senate both are removed from the populace they were to represent. In terms of power, this makes the perpetuity of Milton's assembly quite odious. It was only the infusion of virtue into this body which kept it republican in Milton's mind. Both men held to the conception that the commonwealth was greater than its parts; Hobbes stated that the power of subjects vanished in the presence of the sovereign power.[10] Milton took this position rather in terms of happiness instead of power. The same inductive formula was applied here to different aspects of political theory; the "atheistic" versus the ethical. This was especially obvious in Milton's senate where the accessibility to that body illustrated that the composure of the body itself was greater than its parts. But regardless, Milton's aversion was still to the epitome of the degeneration of all sovereign power, the monarchy:

And why should we disparage and prejudicate our own nation as to fear a scarcity of able and worthy men united in council to govern us, if we will but use diligence and impartiality to find them out and choose them, rather than yoking ourselves to a single person, the natural adversary and oppressor of liberty.[11]

Although a monarchist in his early years Milton was aware that matter and form could not be separated in the political realm in spite of a higher law, in itself apolitical. That was why,

> A commonwealth is to be preferred to a monarchy. Why do more excellent men come from republics than from kingdoms? Because in the former virtue (force) is hindered while in the latter it is feared.[12]

At the very basis of the disagreement between Milton and Hobbes is the role of nature and law and the political deductions attached to their respective positions. While Hobbes differentiated between right and law as the liberty to forbear in antithesis to the power to bind,[13] Milton eschewed all civil law ultimately in favor of Scripture. In place of the civil law, this type of secular antinomianism elevated reason to the apex of its powers, a doctrine Hobbes held as inimical to the commonwealth. Regardless of the apologetics Milton employed in espousing this idea, at the root of it was fear of monarchy, or what Hobbes aptly called "tyrannophobia."

One particular passage in *Leviathan* helps provide an explanation of the inequality of Milton's society. Hobbes saw all men as basically equal in terms of mentality and physical strength by endowment and it was this very equality from which diffidence sprang:

> From this equality of ability, ariseth equality of hope in attaining of our ends. And therefore if any two men desire the same thing, which nevertheless they cannot both enjoy, they become enemies; and in the way to their end, which is principally their own conservation, and sometimes their delectation only, endeavour to destroy or subdue one another.[14]

In Milton's scheme the state of goodness was anterior to Hobbes' idea of the basis of equality and its subsequent inequality. While noting the basis of inequality in Hobbes, it must be noted that it arose with strength and (particularly) mentality to Milton. In order to avoid the secularization Hobbes found necessary to illustrate this incipient state of nature, Milton went one step beyond (or actually prior) to Hobbes and based his society upon goodness. Rather than acknowledging inequality on a secular basis (through physical means) he introduced discord as an extraneous element through the Fall. But the comparison cannot be extended any further between the two since Hobbes conceived of mental endowment as an acquired faculty rather than an innate ability; a position to which Milton was diametrically opposed.

Of Education is central to an understanding of Milton because it illustrates the high position which Milton attributed choice as well as the nature of that choice. Voluntarism was relegated to a secondary position in order to avoid the appetitive. Hobbes would have said that a man called a thing good because he wanted it; his choice lying in the will. Milton, on the other hand, conceived of reason as choice, which ordered the will. As his ethical thought showed, contemplation alone does not make something evil; only when it orders the will does total depravity set in. In cases of religion, only when both reason and the will are affected by erroneous doctrines does true heresy exist. But the will's role should not be denigrated to too great an extent because it was primarily the will which separated the regenerate from the reprobate.

III

Milton's views on toleration were not wholly consistent with his conception of liberty as generally understood. Although freedom of conscience was an inalienable right, it was denied to Catholicism, as mentioned earlier. While the theoretical side of this argument does follow from his delineation of the origins of the freedom of matter, the political ramifications of this denial of toleration prove pernicious to his libertarian thought as a whole. Milton based the denial on what amounted to institutional grounds:

> But as for popery and idolatry, why they also may not hence plead to be tolerated I have much less to say. Their religion the more considered, the less can be acknowledged a religion, but a Roman principality rather, endeavouring to keep up her universal dominion under a new name, and more shadow of a catholic religion; being indeed more rightly named a catholic heresy against the scripture, supported mainly by a civil, and except in Rome, by a foreign power: justly therefor to be suspected, not tolerated, by the magistrate of another country.[15]

Milton was on weak ground here, sounding more like Hobbes in arguing against an institutional religion. What is particularly inconsistent with this position is that by invoking the historical argument accusing the Church of seeking *imperium* as well as *potestas*, Milton assumed that those conceptions of power permeated theological matters rather than being primarily issues of papal foreign policy. It appears that the fear of monarchial religion here forced Milton into an untenable position of not being able to see the forest for the trees in terms of the policies of the Roman Church. Also, the granting of power to the civil magistrate in order to coerce catholicism is something which was otherwise anathema in his thought. In such a manner Milton ferreted out his enemy by pronouncing him secular and remanded him to the authority of the civil power. But Milton was not the tolerationist that Roger Williams or Chilingworth was. He simply bears testimony to the general aphorism that all should be tolerated except those who believe differently from oneself. In a political perspective, this is not toleration as generally conceived of although note must be made of the fear of papal involvement in domestic affairs still prevalent at the time. But Milton was not alone in such an espousal. In an essay entitled "On the Liberty of Conscience" (1660), Henry More stated a similar position. But this magnanimous position was restricted to those who believed in an orthodox conception of God and overtly displayed it. Otherwise the civil magistrate of the nation or the religion could legally restrain the fallen.

The toleration of non-Christians was another matter which does not figure prominently in Milton's thought. Unlike Roger Williams, Milton did not speak decisively concerning the toleration of Jews. This was probably due to the fact that the conflict that affected Milton was Christian in nature and thus he never gave much serious public thought to non-Christians.

The tension which existed in Milton's use of the concept *all* is best evidenced in his *Areopagitica*. In this tract the political syllogism is best put to work to explain what Milton meant by liberty and toleration. Probably the most famous statement concerning liberty in the English language, besides Patrick Henry's, is the following (already mentioned) from the discourse:

> Give me the liberty to know, to utter, and to argue freely according to conscience, above all liberties.[16]

Closer examination of this remark reveals quite a bit about Milton's libertarian views, especially if his later remarks concerning civil power are taken into consideration. In this passage, "give *me* liberty," really should be read "give *me* and *my kind* liberty," and not in a general sense.[17] "Milton's concern here, (and it may be added, in cases like it) is with the crowding of free *consciences* and *Christian* liberties, not *free* consciences and Christian *liberties*."[18] The personal element was too strong to overlook the basis of Milton's private libertarian thought and extend it to all willy-nilly. This is in keeping with the minor premise of his syllogism. This is another reason why Milton's logic was to an extent only interested in argumentation or disposition rather than demonstration. A clear logical demonstration of such a political principle would lead to a clear-cut definitive conception of toleration in all matters of religion and politics; a tenet Milton was not willing to affirm. Milton's free society was therefore not what is generally known today as an open society. *Areopagitica* bears this out. "On one side, it is a plea for the removal of prior restrictions on free expression and on the other an impassioned defense of the *status quo* which Milton was clearly ready to identify with 'true liberty', which he clearly regarded with great satisfaction and which is presupposed in his demand for a press free from prior censorship."[19] *Areopagitica* was not so much a declaration of social progress as a cry for a return to the pre-licensing state of affairs.

Carrying this concept of *we*, a term contrasted with the *they* used to vindicate regicide in the *Tenure of Kings and Magistrates* into the *Commonwealth*, a further and final perspective of the true political *we* is evidenced. In the *Commonwealth* a marked difference is noticeable from the *they* who originally recalled the tyrant and the same *they* that desired a Stuart Restoration:

> . . . if there be a king, which the *inconsiderate multitude* are now so mad upon, mark how far short *we* are like to come of all those happinesses which in a free state *we* shall immediately be possessed of.[20]

This multitude was the same that the king was originally accountable to:

> . . . since the king or magistrate holds his authority of the people, both originally and naturally for *their* good in the first place, and not his own, then may the people, as oft as *they* shall judge it for the best either choose him or reject him.[21]

Through the vacillating use of *we* and *they* Milton interchanged the premises of his syllogism at will to achieve a desired effect. But one fact remains: the concept of *all the people*, which was the basis of his conception of equality, was never used in a functional political manner.

IV

Milton criticism of various types has generally centered around thematic problems in his thought with varying degrees of success. Since his thought is comparatively simple at face value most conclusions reached by scholarship prove more or less correct. One does not have to possess any type of sophisticated training to read and evaluate *Areopagitica* or the treatise on education. But genuine criticism which fails to recognize that Milton's system is one of ethics first and politics subsequently may draw conclusions which contain a modicum of veracity from false premises.

Three fields of criticism are evident in Milton scholarship; the literary, historical, and to a lesser extent, the philosophical. Criticism in the literary area is the most evident but is not the focus of attention here. However, one controversy between literary scholars is particularly relevant to this study and will be briefly examined. Philosophic analysis of Milton is less frequent and usually limited but one of the better known bits of Milton study also bears attention here. The third variety of scholarship usually attempts the widest examination of Milton with usually less than adequate results. This study will concentrate, then, on the arguments and conclusions of C.S. Lewis and T.S. Eliot in literary criticism. A.O. Lovejoy in philosophic analysis, and Don Wolfe in historical study.

In 1936 T.S. Eliot took a position regarding Milton criticism which he later explicated more fully. This renowned remark, from *Milton: Two Studies*, stated that the practitioner of poetry brings to criticism something which the scholar cannot adequately match—an inside knowledge of poetry. This remark has been taken by scholars especially to infer that poets themselves are better critics of poetry than professional critics. In his *Preface to Paradise Lost* C.S. Lewis retaliated with the position that in order to begin criticism, a poet must first ask himself whether he is indeed a poet, thus calling for a critical judgement. His position was that the poet must exercise criticism and beg the question in order to get off the ground in his own particular criticism. But this type of academic sparring was not the point, as Lewis noted, and he extended his argument further in order to prove what he considered the *reductio ad absurdum* of Eliot's position. While this position may be tenable, then, there are certain others which he recognized as less easy to criticize. For instance, the maxim that says only a good man can judge goodness is on more sacrosanct ground and a more appealing notion to offer as evidence. But Lewis concluded that even if this particular maxim were offered in lieu of the remark concerning poets and scholars:

> In the moral sphere, though insight and performance are not strictly equal (which would make both guilt and aspiration impossible), yet it is true that continued disobedience to conscience makes conscience blind. But disobedience to conscience is voluntary; bad poetry on the other hand, is usually not made on purpose. The writer was trying to make good poetry . . . the moral blindness consequent on being a bad man must therefore fall on everyone who is not a good man; whereas the critical blindness (if any) due to being a bad poet need by no means fall on everyone who is not a good poet.[22]

Lewis' point was not well made in this particular context; all he actually proved was that the opposite of good was bad in one place but not necessarily so in the other. But more importantly, he violated two basic Miltonic positions. First, disobedience to conscience may not necessarily be voluntary, it may be emotive as in the case of the man who has no real rational choice to make. Milton's entire philosophy revolved around the necessity of re-opening the avenues of choice and re-instituting that power of choice as reality. Secondly, this criticism violated the basic Miltonic ethical maxim. That statement was relatively terse and strict and although it did admit to knowing something by its opposite, it did expect a sense of regeneration to follow. Eliot's original remarks captured the spirit of Milton precisely. Mr. Lewis' criticism is inappoite to the study of Milton for it does not capture the moralist or poet on his own grounds. As inconsistent as Eliot's position may have been to scholars it was still Milton's position. Lewis' criticism only helped prove that the twentieth century poet's criticism of the seventeenth century was correct in spirit all along.

The method of introducing extraneous material to the study of Milton to serve as an aid can at times be misleading, as the Eliot-Lewis controversy suggests. The concepts of freedom in the state of nature, the quality of matter, basic political inequality, and the ethical orientation of his politics must be understood fully before any contemporary judgements can be superimposed. But even with these facts in mind, a severe mistake may still appear, as one particular historical analysis proves. Don Wolfe's evaluation of Milton in *Milton in the Puritan Revolution* proceeds from a sound basis but adds one element which is extraneous to historical thought in general. Wolfe assumed that democracy was a state of nature, thereby confusing the Aristotelian notion of politics as the master science with the natural order. Although this technique is understandable given the period in which the work was written (1941), it still adds a serious hindrance to the study of Milton.

Wolfe proceeded in his argument using a strong guilt by association instead of a valid historical induction. It does proceed upon a sound knowledge of Milton's ideas but the conclusions reached are not always Miltonic. They rather reflect this strong democratic political allegiance:

> In his belief that there exists a code of abstract justice to all written law superior, that this justice may be understood through man's reason and God's revelation, that any positive law which transgresses the law of nature may be abrogated, that all men are born free, that by the law of nature certain liberties are inailienable, Milton accepts the democratic law of nature.

As has been shown, nothing could be further from the truth than this last line. Wolfe concluded here stating:

> But such an ideal was incapable of realization in actual politics. Milton saw inequality on every hand, concluded with Aristotle that there would always be the ignorant who should be subjected to wiser men, found his countrymen chained by sin and tradition, and in such a mood demanded an aristocracy.[23]

This analysis is only half correct. A democratic law of nature is more verbiage than reality applicable to Milton since the idea was totally alien. Wolfe created a hypallage by deducing a democratic state of nature tainted by inequality which produced an aristocracy out of the Milton position that an aristocratic state of nature tainted by equality in the pristine state produced an inequality. The conclusion reached by Wolfe was partially correct; only the premises were inverted from Milton's original position.

The final evaluation of Milton the political theorist in the same work also suggests a strong historical guilt by association; a guilt

Milton should be acquitted of:

> Milton is entitled to a place as a democratic reformer because in the course of history the liberties for which he stood have gradually become identified with those reforms demanded and achieved by an increasingly large number of voters. The elements of Milton's political philosophy which gave rise to his conception of liberty and which were inherent in the reform movement are his Christian individualism and his sense of abstract justice as embodied in the law of nature.[24]

This conclusion only bears validity through a whig or pragmatist approach to history but is not characteristic of Milton's political philosophy. Quite to the contrary, Milton belonged to a tradition of theo-political thinkers whose immediate academic interest was in the past rather than in the immediate future in a sense of progress. Wolfe's method is not indicative of the spirit of Milton because it simply seeks to superimpose ideas upon him which are inappropriate. While Wolfe would have the reader believe that Milton had an economic philosophy which allied him in spirit with Lilburne and Winstanley (chapter 12) it should be noted that there was absolutely no evidence of economic thought at all in his work. Milton's ideas were borrowed from a great variety of sources and these sources can mutually align him with various groups in a cursory manner. His rejection of the Mosaic law in favor of Scripture shows a hint of antinomianism. The mortalism expressed in the *Christian Doctrine* and the concept of the whole man being the soul was quite similar to the theory advanced by Richard Overton. On the subjects of grace, natural law, and faith he was closely allied with the Cambridge Platonists. But in the final analysis his thought, rooted in antiquity and peppered with contemporary views, remained thoroughly individualistic. While expressing similarities with other groups, he was nevertheless not a Leveller, Cambridge Platonist, Digger, or Fifth Monarchist.

The method of conjecturing an historical contingency in relation to Milton is not characteristic of political and social historians alone but also of the historians of ideas. A.O. Lovejoy attempted such an analysis of Milton through the delineation of what is known as the concept of the "fortunate fall." This enticing idea in Milton is based upon Adam's utterance in Book XII of *Paradise Lost* (473–79):

> Light out of darkness! Full of doubt I stand,
> Whether I should repent me now of sin

> By me done or occasioned, or rejoice
> Much more that much more good thereof shall spring
> To God more glory, more good will to men
> From God—and over wrath grace shall abound.

Through this device Lovejoy conjectured that Milton was expressing the doctrine that the Fall provided a fountainhead of God's grace to mankind which otherwise would not have been made available:

> The Fall could never be sufficiently condemned and lamented; and likewise, when all its consequences were considered, it could never be sufficiently rejoiced over . . . Yet if it had never occurred, the Incarnation and Redemption could never have occurred. These sublime mysteries would have no occasion and no meaning; and therefore the plenitude of the divine greatness and power could neither have been exercised nor have become known to man.[25]

The idea of a *felix culpa* was not a new one, as Lovejoy illustrated. It was evident in the writings of DuBartas, Leo the Great, and Ambrose, among others. But even if it appears to occur in this particular section of the epic, is this interpretation correct with regard to Milton?

Lovejoy concluded that Adam's sin, which was the same sin of his posterity, was the "*conditio sine qua non* both of a greater manifestation of the glory of God and of immeasurably greater benefits for man than could conceivably have been otherwise obtained."[26] Although this essay is not seeking any new interpretations of Milton's epic, it must be said that this conclusion is not in accord with Milton's own philosophic thought. Whatever may have been the positive consequences of the Fall, they cannot be compared to the pristine bliss of the prelapsarian state; miracles notwithstanding. But this is not the primary point of criticism. A return to an already quoted excerpt from the *Art of Logic* will illustrate:

> Hence it is understood that the cause *sine qua non*, as it is commonly called, is improperly and as though fortuitously considered a cause, as when the loss of something is called the cause of its finding, since loss of necessity precedes finding.[27]

The Fall could not have been a cause of further grace since it did not efficiently precede the alleged effect. Closer to the text of the epic is probably the mood of Adam which tried to rationalize his deed rather than rejoice in it. But even by leaving his logic aside, the idea of the

Fall as a necessary element in Milton's thought can only be valid in a negative manner for the sake of illustration. The Fall was an historical event which first illustrated the weakness of the will and the appetitive propensity of man: it was not an historical occasion upon which Milton sought to build a concept of history or even a social philosophy. There is little evidence to support Lovejoy's assertion although the idea is an attractive one nevertheless. But the true meaning of such an idea is not to be found by comparing Milton to anyone else under the panache of the history of ideas when internal evidence supports the opposite.

Criticism of Milton critics does not aid in explaining the inconsistencies of significant political importance in his thought. The question remains of why Milton made such obvious errors in regard to basic political doctrines as equality and political participation. And of more significance is the related question of why it requires such a close scrutiny to put together the pieces of what must be considered a significant political philosophy. One possible solution may be suggested by the persecution thesis of Leo Strauss. According to Strauss, if an author makes a flagrant mistake which seems to betray his intelligence, one may possibly suspect an esoteric form of writing evident along with the exoteric.[28] A plausible reason for this would be extraneous pressure which did not enable the writer to express himself fully for fear of some form of persecution. Now certain aspects of Milton's career fit this categorization. As Masson noted, in spite of the regicide tracts (*Tenure of Kings and Magistrates* and *Eikonoklastes* especially) Milton's name was not included in the Indemnity Act of 1660 and he emerged unscathed from the Stuart Restoration.[29] It was probably this extraordinary piece of luck, which did not fall on Harrington, that made Milton all the wiser concerning publication of any further unorthodox ideas. As noted earlier, the *Christian Doctrine* was not discovered and published until 1823. But all of Milton's major political works were published prior to 1660. Is, then, the persecution thesis of any value in explaining his purely political thought? The least that may be conjectured in this respect is that Milton did obviously pay lip service to some popular doctrines. It would have have been feasible to foster a theo-political philosophy on one hand and maintain that each man was the interpreter of his own faith on the other. Like Hobbes, Milton took certain doctrines for granted when he expounded his ideas. Equality in the pristine sense was one of them. Thus, the remark concerning basic equality in the *Tenure of Kings and Magistrates*, which implied much but actually stated little, may have been no more than a courteous bow to his contemporary theorists who did expound more radical political and social ideas. And whether or not Milton's ideas remained constant to the extent that historical development of them is somewhat supererogatory is a problem for his biographers, although this study has considered them as basically constant. But conjecture of this type does achieve one important insight. It serves to remind the student of Milton that if there is a suspicion that a is not b even though it was stated as such, and even if there is no sound historical evidence to underwrite the opposite, the tension should not be written off as merely intuitive knowledge. Neither is there any corroborative evidence to blindly support Mr Lewis' assertion that bad poetry (or any literary endeavour for that matter) is usually not made on purpose.

Little is left to be said of Milton's political thought. Politics and poetry met in his thought on the level of theology which, in retrospect, made all human endeavour and institutions subservient and ministerial to its eschatology. What was not achieved in his prose was certainly achieved through his later poetry, the product of the mature Milton. His lasting contribution to political theory was the revival of the classical paradigm of the mixed regime in its purist form before it subsequently succumbed to the empiricists. Perhaps the tersest phrase by which his political philosophy will be remembered is that aphorism best enunciated by Thoreau: that government is best which governs least.

NOTES

1. *Works* XI, p. 71.
2. Based upon *Art of Logic*, *Works* XI, p. 401.
3. A. Fields, "Milton and Self-Knowledge," PMLA, LXXXIII (1968), 394.
4. *Hughes*, p. 895.
5. V 486–490.
6. *Leviathan*, ed. Michael Oakeshott (Oxford, 1957), chap. 17.
7. *Ibid.*, chap. 29.
8. *Ibid.*, chap. 43.
9. *Works* III, p. 69.
10. *Leviathan*, chap. 18.
11. *Hughes*, p. 893.
12. *Works* XVIII, p. 164.
13. *Leviathan*, chap. 14.
14. *Ibid.*, chap. 13.
15. *Hughes*, p. 846.
16. *Ibid.*, p. 746.

17. W. Kendall, "How to Read Milton's *Areopagitica*," *JP*, XXII (1960), 447.
18. *Ibid.*, p. 453.
19. *Ibid.*, p. 463.
20. *Hughes*, p. 892; my italics.
21. *Ibid.*, p. 757; my italics.
22. Lewis, *op. cit.*, pp. 10 f.
23. *Milton in the Puritan Revolution*, p. 332.
24. *Ibid.*, p. 336.
25. A.O. Lovejoy, "Milton and the Paradox of the Fortunate Fall," *Essays in the History of Ideas* (Baltimore, 1948), 278.
26. *Ibid.*, pp. 278 f.
27. *Works* XI, pp. 29 f.
28. Leo Strauss, *Persecution and the Art of Writing* (Glencoe, Illinois, 1952), p. 24.
29. *Life of Milton*, vol. VI, pp. 162 ff.

Appendix I
The Problem of *Essence*

The theology of Origen was quite similar to that posited in Milton's cosmology in that both adopted a Platonic chain of being which originated in the Godhead. It was to this position and the conclusions drawn from it that Milton owed his greatest debt to Origen's system. The speculative theology of Arius, on the other hand, also had its attraction for Milton but there appear to be certain tenets in the Arian creed which Milton did not accept.

Origen's work has been preserved in part through the Latin and Greek of St. Jerome and in a selection of his works published by St. Basil. Very little of Arius' teaching has survived in extant form. Both owe the preservation of their teachings in some way to the Church although a negative factor is evident here, especially in the case of Arius.

Origen conceived of the Father as the ultimate and unmoved goodness. In relation to him the Son or *Logos* was a subordinate person with a different essence. The same was true of the Holy Spirit, who was subordinate to both Father and Son. The inequality of the three persons was based upon gradations of essence. The Son served a functional role as the *Logos*, a mediator between the unity of God and the multiplicity of his beings.[1] The Son thus had a twofold aspect; one in relation to God and the other to corporeal beings.

The doctrine of Origen's Trinity is commonly known as the heresy of subordinationism, i.e. while not denying that there are three persons in the Trinity it does deny their equality on the basis of essence. Equality of essence in the Trinity was confirmed at the Council of Nicea in 325 in refute to the teachings of Arius.

Arius extended this anti-Trinitarian position by denying that the Son was God. The Godhead was conceived of as unique, transcendent, and indivisible with its essence not capable of being shared or communicated.[2] The Son and Holy Spirit were not of the same essence or substance as the Father and were created *ex nihilo* by his will. Even though having created the Son, the Father remained incommunicable to him.

The difference between these two creeds and their relation to Milton evolves around the semantical problem of what was meant by the terms *essence* and *substance*. As has been shown in Chapter 2, Milton denied the essential quality of the three persons but did not deny their consubstantiality, or sharing in the substratum of the Godhead. Thus, while possessing different essences the Son and Holy Spirit still shared in the substance of the Father. In this way, Arianism would be denied but subordinationism still maintained. This was given further credence by Milton's delineation of the ideas of form and matter in the *Art of Logic*. All things are able to share in the same generic stuff of matter and still possess their own individual personalities or forms. The two are inseparable but yet distinct. "For when the essence of almost anything is partly common, partly proper, the matter constitutes what is common, the form what is proper.[3] The three persons could be conceived of as sharing the same matter, or being consubstantial,[4] while the essence of each person or member still retained its individuality.

NOTES

1. J.N.D. Kelly, *Early Christian Doctrines*, p. 128.
2. *Ibid.*, p. 227.
3. *Works* XI, p. 39.
4. This point was originally made by W.B. Hunter in "Some Problems in John Milton's Theological Vocabulary," *HTR*, LVII (1964).

Appendix II
Hartlib and Comenius

Hartlib and Comenius were the two outstanding advocates of educational reform in the first half of the seventeenth century. They both embraced the same common ideals and educational philosophy termed pansophy. Milton's philosophic relationship with the two has been discussed earlier but the social relationship that existed between him and Hartlib is not exactly clear. The three, however, agree with regard to common goals.

Hartlib was born around 1600 in Elbing in Poland and emigrated to Prussia at an early age to avoid religious persecution. He eventually found his way to England and took up studies at Cambridge in 1625, which was the first year of Milton's matriculation. During this period he avowedly embraced the pansophic principles of Comenius and gathered around himself a circle of educational theorists who shared his penchant for pansophy, among them John Dury, Cheyney Culpeper, and John Pell. His major life project was the hope of attaining a college of pansophic principles centered in either London or Oxford. The Root and Branch Petition of 1640, which would have abolished church schools, gave him great hope that the time for educational reform was imminent. However, the failure of the bill to materialize as well as the cold reception to the pansophic college marked the defeat of his hope of establishing this theoretical system on a universal scale in England, although a pansophic clearinghouse of sorts was opened on the continent. He died in poverty in 1662 after leading a life contrasted by wealth as well as penury.

Hartlib's most famous works include *A Description of the Famous Kingdome of Macaria* (1641), *Englands Thankfulnesse* (1642), *Englands Reformation* (1647), and the *True and Readie Way to Learne the Latin Tongue* (1645) plus divers works on husbandry. Masson remarked:

> By the common consent of all who have explored the intellectual and social history of England in the seventeenth century, he is one of the most interesting and memorable figures of that whole period.

Appendix II — Hartlib and Comenius

He is interesting both for what he did himself and also on account of the number and intimacy of his contacts with other interesting people.[1]

Oddly enough, although Milton addressed his educational tract to him, nothing in the remains of Hartlib's papers originated from Milton and neither was there a copy of *Of Education* in his correspondence.[2]

Comenius was born John Amos Komensky in Comnia, Moravia in 1592. Perhaps his flair for the academic can best be seen in the latinization of his name into Joannus Amosius Comenius. He took up various experimental teaching projects in his native area and gained a worldwide reputation for his *Janua Linguarum Reserata*, or the *Gate of Languages Opened*, popularizing an area of instruction theory which was equally shared by Dury, Hartlib, and Milton in later years. Since the publication of this work, Comenius had been in touch with Hartlib in England.[3]

Comenius is best known for his *Didactica Magna (Great Didactic)* which proposed the universal content of his philosophic system, the *Via Lucis (Way of Light)* which moved strongly toward chiliastic ends, and the *Reformation of Schooles*, an abridgement of the *Didactica* into English by Hartlib. The *Didactica* was written in 1629 and enlarged in 1638 at the bequest of the government of Sweden after Comenius had first refused its offer to emigrate and aid in the reform of Swedish education. His works were translated into many languages and he may well have been one of the most widely read men of his century.

In contrast to the scholarship of Milton's tract on education, the writings of Hartlib and Comenius were rather in the realm of the popular. Both adopted ideas which were intended for popular dissemination rather than known for their logical arguments or epistemological appeal. This may well add to the explanation of why Milton was not aligned with them other than in a casual manner.

NOTES

1. *Life of Milton*, III, p. 194.
2. G.H. Turnbull, *Hartlib, Dury, and Comenius* (Liverpool, 1947), p. 44.
3. Masson, *op. cit.*, p. 202.

Appendix III
Filmer's Critique of Milton

Sir Robert Filmer's criticism of Milton's theory of the political contract and the regicide was published in 1652 along with essays on Grotius and Hobbes, under the title of *Observations Concerning the Original of Government*. This criticism was based upon the theory of government expounded in *Patriarcha*, the classic of absolutist theory first published in 1680 but in circulation for several decades prior.

Patriarcha advanced the theory that all government had evolved unchanged from the state of nature characterized by Adam's patriarchal dominion over all things. This God-given state of filial subservance was basic to all society:

> I see not then how the children of Adam, or of any man else, can be free from subjection to their parents. And this subordination of children is the fountain of all regal authority, by the ordination of God himself.[1]

This unbroken chain of unimpeded authoritarian monarchy had never been abrogated in the course of history; neither by any sort of contract between the people and monarch or even by the post-deluvian dispersement of Noah's sons.[2] Upon this simple foundation followed all subsequent political corollaries.

The concept of freedom was permeated by this condition. No equality was evident in the freedom of nature. All men were born free of the master-subject relationship but not of the filial: "No man is born a servant or subject to the power of a master by the law of nature, yet every man is born subject to the power of a Father."[3] Filmer's documentation of this position was somewhat unique. He ascribed the filial-political relationship under the form of monarchy as the best form of government in Aristotle's opinion. When Aristotle mentioned equality of mankind in the *Politics*, he was merely relating the position of others: when he spoke of monarchy as the truest form of government he uttered his own opinion.[4] This was Filmer's interpretation of what is generally known as Aristotle's inductive method whereby he traced government from the simplest to the most sophisticated form of political society then known. This analysis was expanded in his *Observations Upon Aristotle's Politics Touching Forms of Government*, c. 1652. Filmer hoped to enlist Aristotle as an authority in the royalist cause against the parliamentarians.

The rule of the multitude was discounted as dysfunctional. Besides violating the patriarchal state of nature the entire populace could not in effect rule themselves:

> Therefore, unless it can be proved by some law of nature that the major, or some other part, have power to overrule the rest of the multitude, it must follow that the acts of the multitude not entire are not binding to all, but only to such as consent to them.[5]

To bolster this argument, Filmer quoted Aristotle in the *Nicomachean Ethics* to prove that "monarchy is the best form of government, and a popular estate the worst."[6] This quote by Filmer was correct but what he failed to recognize was Aristotle's concept that the perversion of kingship as the best form into tyranny was the worst possible form conceivable.[7] In such a manner democracy could not be introduced into a kingdom without causing chaos. At best, it could only adequately serve a city.

The patriarch was naturally not subject to the common or civil laws but was rather their embodiment. The monarch, as Father, ruled by his own volition and not by his children's. This was based upon a facile historical proof:

> A proof unanswerable for the superiority of Princes above laws is this, that there were kings before there were any laws. For a long time the word of the king was the only law.[8]

The king was then also the source of law, a power passed down through the generations. Laws themselves were only a matter of expediency. After society had become too large to enable a king to personally adjudicate for his subjects individually, laws came into existence out of necessity but were still derivative of the king's will. Any liberty which accrued to the people was still based upon the approbation of the monarch and not any law of nature which granted power to the people. The father figure remained supreme and the fountainhead of all liberties.

This was the theory behind the criticism of Milton as found in

"Observations on Mr. Milton Against Salamasius." The critique is not especially informative or cogent but it does make several interesting points in relation to Milton's weak spots, which Filmer readily detected. The initial criticism levelled was in relation to Milton's elitist doctrine of the ruling class:

> ... nay J.M. will not allow the major part of the representors to be the people but the sounder and better part only of them, and in right down terms he tells us to determine who is a tyrannt, he leaves to the magistrates at least to the uprighter sort of them and of the people, though in less number by many to judge as they find cause. If the sounder, the better, and the uprighter part have the power of the people, how shall we know, or who shall judge who they be?[9]

This was aimed at Milton's pronouncements in the *First Defense* against Salamasius. Filmer immediately detected Milton's ambivalence in the use of the term people, an attack he continued later in the short pamphlet. But the real dispute between the two was not over matters concerning the people or the efficiency of governments but in two more substantive areas. The first concerned Filmer's concept of *jus regni* and his denial of natural law knowable to the individual.

By placing the monarch above all law Filmer effectively destroyed any norm to which society could adhere other than the king's will:

> ... humane laws must not be shuffled in with divine, they are not of the same authority: if humane laws bind a King, it is impossible for him to have supreme power amongst men.[10]

Milton's conception of reason played no role in Filmer's theory and he thereby avoided the necessity of vindicating omnipotent monarchy in the face of it.

Filmer's understanding of Milton's idea of kingship was essentially correct:

> He is the one to whom the people gave power to see that nothing be done against the law, and that he keep our laws, and not impose his own. Whereas all other men have the faculty of seeing by nature, the king only hath it by the gift of the people, other power he had none; he may see the judges keep the laws if they will; he cannot compel them, for he may not imprison, fine, nor punish any man.[11]

Appendix III — Filmer's Critique of Milton 113

Milton's position stated that the king was the first able man to be found in society who took the reins of government: Filmer's was that the law of nature dictated this position, able or not. Liberty to Filmer was nothing more than an arbitrary gift; quite a difference from that of the ideas found in *Areopagitica*. But one point of his criticism proved most trenchant in relation to Milton:

> If almost all liberty be in choosing of the kind of government, the people have a poor bargain of it, who cannot exercise their liberty, but in chopping and changing their government, and have liberty only to give away liberty, than which there is not a greater mischief, as being the cause of endless sedition.[12]

This was actually the only political liberty Milton granted to the people as a whole. And obviously in time of tranquility not much liberty was to be realized based upon the ideas later expounded in the *Commonwealth*.

The second major difference between the two arises from Filmer's conception of the relation of power and the form of government. In antithesis to Milton, who held that the form of government reflected either a healthy or diseased polity, Filmer contended that ". . . it doth not follow that the form of government is, or can be in its own nature ill, because the governor is so."[13] Continued bad experience with a monarchy did not necessarily imply that monarchy itself was bad. But to Milton, a diseased head meant a diseased body. Waiting for an odious king to die in order to take a chance with a new one was not the natural way for governments to progress.

Milton and Filmer represent the opposites of the "Adam theorists." In retrospect, Milton held a more sophisticated conception of government evolving from Adam than did Filmer. The apologetic nature of *Patriarcha* was far removed from any idea of political realism and made even Hobbes' conception of indivisible sovereignty look pale in comparison. And his critique of Milton in the brief nine pages which it comprises did not come to grips with the complete Milton, who was in evidence at the time of the critique. Filmer's real misunderstanding of Milton is obvious in the last paragraph of the work:

> It is well said by J.M. that all liberty doth almost consist in choosing their form of government, for there is another liberty exercised by the people, which he mentions not, which is the liberty of the peoples choosing their religion.

NOTES

1. Robert Filmer, *Patriarcha and Other Political Writings*, ed. Peter Laslett (Oxford, 1949), p. 57.
2. *Ibid.*, p. 64.
3. *Ibid.*, p. 74.
4. *Ibid.*, p. 79.
5. *Ibid.*, p. 82.
6. *Ibid.*, p. 85.
7. See *Ethics* 1160 b.
8. *Patriarcha*, p. 96.
9. *Ibid.*, p. 252.
10. *Ibid.*, p. 254.
11. *Ibid.*, p. 255.
12. *Ibid.*, p. 256.
13. *Ibid.*, p. 259.

Bibliography

BOOKS

Agar, Herbert. *Milton and Plato* (Princeton, 1928).
Ainsworth, O. *Milton on Education* (New Haven, 1928).
Allen, J.W. *English Political Thought, 1603–1644* (London, 1938).
Aristotle. *Nicomachean Ethics*, trans. M. Oswald (New York, 1962).
———. *Politics*, trans. Ernest Barker (Oxford, 1960).
———. *Rhetoric*, trans. W. Roberts (New York, 1954).
Arthos, John. *Milton and the Italian Cities* (London, 1968).
Augustine. *City of God Against the Pagans*, trans. P. Levine (London, 1966).
———. *Confessions*, trans. E. Pusey (New York, 1949).
Austin, E. *The Ethics of the Cambridge Platonists* (University of Pennsylvania, 1935).
Barker, Arthur. *Milton and the Puritan Dilemma* (Toronto, 1942).
Blitzer, Charles. *An Immortal Commonwealth: The Political Thought of James Harrington* (New Haven, 1960).
Butcher, S.H. (trans.) *Aristotle's Theory of Poetry and Fine Art* (New York, 1951).
Cicero. *De Re Publica and De Legibus*, trans. C.W. Keyes (London, 1970).
Clark, D. *John Milton at St. Paul's School* (New York, 1948).
Comenius. *Great Didactic*, trans. M. Keatinge (London, 1923).
———. *Reformation of Schooles* (London, 1642), facsimile reprint 1969.
Cragg, G. (ed.) *The Cambridge Platonists* (New York, 1968).
Curry, W.C. *Milton's Ontology, Cosmogony, and Physics* (Lexington, Kentucky, 1957).
Daiches, D. *Milton* (London, 1957).
Darbishire, H. (ed.) *Early Lives of Milton* (London, 1932).
DeSelincourt, E. *English Poets and the National Idea* (Oxford, 1915).
Dunning, W.A. *A History of Political Ideas: From Luther to Montesquieu* (London, 1959).
Dury, John. *A motion tending to the publick good* (London, 1642).

———. *The Reformed School* (London, n.d.).
Eastland, E. *Milton's Ethics* (Nashville, 1942).
Eliot, T.S. *Milton: Two Studies* (London, 1968).
Filmer, Robert. *Patriarcha and Other Political Writings* ed. P. Laslett (Oxford, 1949).
Fink, Z.S. *The Classical Republicans* (Evanston, 1945).
Fixler, M. *Milton and the Kingdoms of God* (London, 1964).
Gilman, W.E. *Milton's Rhetoric* (Columbia, Mo., 1939).
Gooch, G.P. *English Democratic Ideas in the Seventeenth Century* (Cambridge, 1954).
Gough, J.W. *The Social Contract* (Oxford, 1957).
Grace, W. *Ideas in Milton* (University of Notre Dame, 1968).
Hanford, J.H. *A Milton Handbook* (New York, 1946).
Harrington, James. *Oceana and Other Works* (London, 1771).
———. *Political Writings*, ed. C. Blitzer (New York, 1955).
Hartlib, S. *Considerations tending to the happy accomplishment of England's reformation in Church and State* (London, 1647).
———. *A description of the famous kingdome of Macaria* (London, 1641).
———. *The True and Readie Way to Learne the Latine Tongue* (London, 1654).
Hesselberg, A. *A Comparative Study of Milton and Molina* (Washington, 1952).
Hill, C. *Intellectual Origins of the English Revolution* (Oxford, 1965).
———. *Milton and the English Revolution* (London, 1977).
Hobbes, Thomas. *Leviathan*, ed. M. Oakeshott (Oxford, 1957).
Howell, W. *Logic and Rhetoric in England, 1500–1700* (Princeton, 1956).
Hughes, M. *Ten Perspectives on Milton* (New Haven and London, 1965).
An Index to the Columbia Edition of the Works of Milton, ed. F. Patterson (New York, 1940).
Kelley, Maurice. *This Great Argument* (Gloucester, Mass., 1962).
Kelly, J.N.D. *Early Christian Doctrines* (London, 1958).
Krouse, F.M. *Milton's Samson and the Christian Tradition* (Princeton, 1949).
Langdon, Ida. *Milton's Theory of Poetry and Fine Art* (New Haven, 1924).
LeComte, E.S. *A Milton Dictionary* (London, 1961).
Lessing, G.E. *Hamburg Dramaturgy*, trans. H. Zimmern (New York, 1962).
Lewis, C.S. *A Preface to Paradise Lost* (Oxford, 1967).

Madsen, W. *From Shadowy Types to Truth* (New Haven, 1968).
Masson, David. *The Life of Milton*, in six volumes (Cambridge, Mass. and London, 1859).
Milton, John. *Complete Poems and Major Prose*, ed. M. Hughes (New York, 1957).
———. *The Works of John Milton*, ed. F. Patterson, 18 vols. in 21 (New York, 1931–38).
———. *The Ready and Easy Way to Establish a Free Commonwealth*, ed. E.M. Clark (New Haven, 1915).
———. *Private Correspondence and Academic Exercises* trans. P. Tillyard (Cambridge, 1932).
Morrison, W. *Milton and Liberty* (London, 1909),
New Catholic Encyclopedia, in fifteen volumes (New York and London, 1967).
Parker, W.R. *Milton's Debt to Greek Tragedy in Samson Agonistes* (Baltimore, 1937).
Patrides, C.A. *Milton and the Christian Tradition* (Oxford, 1966).
Plato. *The Laws*, trans. B. Jowett (Oxford, 1968).
———. *The Republic*, trans. F. Cornford (Oxford, 1968).
Polybius. *The Histories*, trans. W. Paton (London, 1923).
Powicke, F. *The Cambridge Platonists* (London, 1926).
Raymond, Dora. *Oliver's Secretary* (New York, 1932).
Robins, Harry. *If This Be Heresy: A Study of Milton and Origen* (Urbana, 1962).
Ross, M. *Milton's Royalism* (Ithaca, 1943).
Samuel, Irene. *Plato and Milton* (Ithaca, 1947).
Saurat, Denis. *Milton: Man and Thinker* (London, 1946).
Schultz, H. *Milton and Forbidden Knowledge* (New York, 1955).
Sensabaugh, G. *That Grand Whig Milton* (Stanford, 1952).
Sewell, A. *A Study of Milton's Christian Doctrine* (Oxford, 1939).
Sidney, Philip. *Complete Works*, vol. III (Cambridge, 1923).
Strauss, Leo. *On Tyranny* (Glencoe, Illinois, 1963).
———. *Persecution and the Art of Writing* (Glencoe, 1952).
Thorpe, J. *Milton Criticism From Four Centuries* (London, 1951).
Tillyard, E.M.W. *Milton* (New York, 1966).
———. *Studies in Milton* (London, 1951).
Turnbull, G. *Hartlib, Dury, and Comenius* (Liverpool, 1947).
Waldock, A.J. *Paradise Lost and its Critics* (Cambridge, 1964).
Webster, Charles. (ed.) *Samuel Hartlib and the Advancement of Learning* (Cambridge, 1970).
Williams, Norman P. *The Ideas of the Fall and of Original Sin* (London, 1929).

Wolfe, Don. *Milton in the Puritan Revolution* (New York, 1962).
Wood, Louis. *The Form and Origin of Milton's Antitrinitarian Conception* (London, Ontario, 1911).
Zagorin, Perez. *A History of Political Thought in the English Revolution* (London, 1954).

ARTICLES

Adamson, J.H., "Milton's Arianism," *HTR*, LIII (1960), 269–276.
————., "Milton and the Creation," *JEGP*, LXI (1962) 756–778.
Barker, A., "Christian Liberty in Milton's Divorce Pamphlets," *MLR*, XXXV (1940), 153–161.
Boswell, J.C., "Milton and Prevenient Grace," *SEL*, VII (1967), 83–94.
Broadbent, J.B., "Milton's Rhetoric," *MP*, LVI (1958), 224–242.
Bryant, Joseph, "A Reply to 'Milton's Moscovia Not History,'" *PQ*, XXXI (1952), 221–223.
————., "Milton and the Art of History: A Study of Two Influences on *A Brief History of Moscovia*," *PQ* XXIX (1950), 15–30.
Bundy, M.W., "Milton's View of Education in *Paradise Lost*," *JEGP*, XXI (1922), 127–152.
Berns, Walter, "John Milton," *A History of Political Philosophy*, ed. Leo Strauss and J. Cropsey (Chicago, 1963), 397–412.
Bywater, I., "Milton and the Aristotelian Definition of Tragedy," *JPh*, XXVII (1901).
Duhamel, P., "Milton's Alleged Ramism," *PMLA*, LXVII (1952), 1035–1053.
Duvall, R.F., "Time, Place, Persons: The Background for Milton's *Of Reformation*," *SEL*, VII (1967), 106–118.
Fields, A., "Milton and Self-Knowledge," *PMLA*, LXXXIII (1968), 392–399.
Fink, Z.S., "The Development of Milton's Political Thought," *PMLA*, LVII (1942), 705–736.
————., Political Implications of *Paradise Regained*," *JEGP*, XL (1941), 482–488.
Firth, C.H., "Milton as Historian," *Proceedings of the British Academy*, III (1907).
Fisher, Peter, "Milton's Logic," *JHI*, XXIII (1962), 37–60.
Fogle, French, "Milton as Historian," *Milton and Clarendon* (Los Angeles, 1965), 1–18.

French, J.M., "Milton as a Historian," *PMLA*, L (1935), 469–479.

———., "Some Notes on Milton's *Accedence Commenc't Grammar*," *JEGP*, LX (1961), 641–650.

Gilbert, A.H., "Aristotle's *Ton Omoion*, (*Poetics* 13.53 a5)," *SP*, LVI (1959), 1–7.

Gleason, J.R., "The Nature of Milton's Moscovia," *SP*, LXI (1964), 640–649.

Gossman, Ann, "Milton's Samson as the Tragic Hero Purified by Trial," *JEGP*, LXI (1962), 528–541.

Grace, William, "Milton, Salamasius, and the Natural Law," *JHI*, XXIV (1963), 323–336.

Haller, W., "Before *Areopagitica*," *PMLA*, XLII (1927), 875–900.

———., "Milton and the Protestant Ethic," *JBS*, I (1961), 52–57.

Hanford, J.H., "Milton and the Art of War," *SP*, XVIII (1921), 232–266.

Henry, N.H., "Milton and Hobbes: Mortalism and the Intermediate State," *SP*, XLVIII (1951), 234–249.

———., "Milton's Last Pamphlet: Theocrasy and Intolerance," *A Tribute to George Coffin Taylor* (Chapel Hill, 1952), 197—210.

Hughes, M., "Three Issues of Principle," *Complete Prose of John Milton*, Vol. III (New Haven, 1962), 65–100.

Hunter, W.B., "Milton's Arianism Reconsidered," *HTR*, LII (1959), 9—35.

———., "Milton's Materialistic Life Principle," *JEGP*, XLV (1946), 68–76.

———., "Milton's Power of Matter," *JHI*, XIII (1952) 551–562.

———., "Milton and the Waldensians," *SEL*, XI (1971), 153–164.

———., "Some Problems in John Milton's Theological Vocabulary," *HTR*, LVII (1964), 335–365.

Huntley, John, "*Proairesis*, Synteresis, and the Ethical Orientation of Milton's *Of Education*," *PQ*, XLIII (1964), 40–46.

Kelley, M., "Milton's Arianism Again Reconsidered," *HTR*, LIV (1961), 192–205.

———., "Milton and the Third Person of the Trinity," *PQ*, XXIX (1950), 15–30.

Kendall, W., "How to Read Milton's *Areopagitica*," *JP*, XXII (1960), 439–473.

Leach, A.F., "Milton as a Schoolboy and Schoolmaster," *Proceedings of the British Academy* III (1907).

Lewalski, B., "Milton on Learning and the Learned-Ministry Controversy," *HLQ*, XXIV (1961), 267–281.

———., "Milton: Political Beliefs and Polemical Methods," *PMLA*, LXXIV (1959), 191–202.
Lovejoy, A.O., "Milton and the Paradox of the Fortunate Fall," *Essays in the History of Ideas* (Baltimore, 1948), 277–295.
Mack, J.F., "The Evolution of Milton's Political Thinking," *SR*, XXX (1922), 193–205.
Mueller, M., "Sixteenth Century Italian Criticism and Milton's Theory of Catharsis, *SEL*, VI (1966), 139–150.
Newmann, J.H., "Milton's Prose Vocabulary," *PMLA*, LX (1948), 102–120.
Nicolson, Marjorie, "Milton and Hobbes," *SP*, XXIII (1926), 405–433.
———., "The Spirit World of Milton and More," *SP*, XXII (1925), 433–452.
Parks, G.B., "Milton's Moscovia Not History," *PQ*, XXI (1952), 218–221.
Patrides, C.A., "Milton and Arianism," *JHI*, XXV (1964), 423–429.
———., "Milton and the Protestant Theory of the Atonement," *PMLA*, LXXIV (1959), 7–13.
Rice, Warner, "A Note on *Areopagitica*," *JEGP*, XL (1941), 474–484.
Scott, W., "Ramism and Milton's Concept of Poetic Fancy," *PQ*, XLII (1963), 183–189.
Sellin, Paul, "Sources of Milton's Catharsis: A Reconsideration," *JEGP* LX (1941), 712–730.
Sensabaugh, G., "Milton on Learning," *SP*, XLIII (1946), 258–272.
Sewell, A., "Milton and the Mosaic Law," *MLR*, XXX (1935), 13–18.
Sirluck, E., "Milton's Political Thought: The First Cycle," *MP*, LXI (1964), 209–224.
———., "Of Education," *Complete Prose Works of John Milton*, Vol. II (New Haven, 1959), 184–216.
Smith, C.I., "Some Ideas on Education Before Locke," *JHI*, XXIII (1962), 403–406.
Stapleton, L., "Milton's Conception of Time in the *Christian Doctrine*," *HTR*, LVII (1964), 9–21.
Thompson, E.N., "Milton's *Of Education*," *SP*, XV (1918), 159–175.
Whiting, G., "The Sources of *Eikonoklastes*: A Resurvey," *SP*, XXXII (1935), 74–102.
Williamson, G., "Milton and the Moralist Heresy," *SP*, XXXII (1935), 553–579.

———., "The Education of Adam," *MP*, LXI (1963), 96–109.
Wolfe, Don, "Limits of Miltonic Toleration," *JEGP*, LX (1961) 834–846.
———., "Milton's Conception of Ruler," *SP*, XXIII (1936), 253–272.
———., "Milton and Hobbes," *SP*, XLI (1944), 410–426.
———., "Milton, Lilburne, and the People," *MP*, XXXI (1934), 253–272.
———., "The Role of Milton's Christ," *SR*, LI (1943), 467–475.
Woodhouse, A.S.P., "Milton, Puritanism, and Liberty," *UTQ*, IV (1935), 1–18.

Index

Acts of the Apostles 22
Adams, John 78
Aristotle 8, 13, 53, 57, 65, 75, 78, 79, 100
  Ethics 14
  on education 54, 62
  on justice 14–15, 82
  on knowledge in rulers and citizens 12
  Poetics 47
  Politics 15, 54, 63, 65, 80
Arius 31
Augustinianism 7

Bede 48

Calvinism 25
Cambridge Platonists 7, 85, 91, 101
Charles I 75
Cicero 78
Comenius, John Amos 40, 55
  Didactica 53, 57
  pansophy of 53
  Reformation of Schooles 53
Commonwealth, Milton's
  coercion in 74–6
  concept of whole people 71–2
  dictatorial powers in 82
  education in 54
  expression of political principles 71
  idea of perpetual council or senate in 78–83, 88, 93
  law in 82
  local government 81, 83, 88
  moral covenant in 77
  nature of citizen in 83, 84–5
  oligarchic rule 80
  political freedom and the Fall 72–4
  Ready and Easy Way to Establish a Free Commonwealth 22, 56, 63, 68, 71, 72, 78, 81, 82, 90, 91, 97
  religious nature of 44, 72, 76
Conscience 21–2
Constantine, Emperor 31
Cromwell, Oliver 45, 59
Cudworth, Ralph 7
  attacks Hobbes 6
Culpeper, Cheyney
  on Milton's *Of Education* 53

Dury, John 40
  Reformed School 55, 57, 59

Education, Milton's view of 40, 41, 52, 68–9, 88
  academy for 59

Index

aim of learning 57
Aristotelian framework 54, 60, 62–3
arts and sciences 55
authorities behind 53
basis of theory 59
defined 29
diet 66–7
element of *proairesis* 59, 60, 62, 63, 66, 90
elements of Platonism 54, 58, 60, 61, 62, 66
intrinsic part of liberty 56
knowledge of Latin 56, 57
music in 65, 66
Of Education 11, 23, 47, 49, 52, 52–3, 54, 55, 56, 62, 68, 71, 83, 90, 95
question of pupils seeing comedies and tragedies 65–6
reading and studies 62–3, 64–5
travel abroad 66
university teaching errors 58
Eliot, T. S.
literary criticism of Milton 98, 99
Milton: Two Studies 98

Fink, Z. S. 81
Firth, C. H. 48

Harrington, James 82, 85, 103
Oceana 78, 79
Hartlib, S. 5, 40, 53, 55, 58, 67
True and Readie Way to Learn the Latin Tongue 57

Henry, Patrick 96
History, Milton's concept of 39, 46, 49
"didactic experience" 39, 49–50
elements of nobility and virtue in 43
historical method 43–4
History of Britain 48, 49, 50
History of Muscovy 49
"mode of behaviour" 39, 40, 50
role in education 41
"yoke" concept 48
Hobbes, Thomas 46, 75, 85, 90, 96, 103
Leviathan 94
on law in the commonwealth 92
on monarchy 92, 93
philosophy compared with Milton's 91–5
villainizing of man's nature in 6, 7
Hughes, Merritt 40

Jowett, Benjamin 56

Laud, Archbishop 35
Lewis, C. S. 104
answers T. S. Eliot on Milton 98–9
Preface to Paradise Lost 98
Lilburne, John 101
Lovejoy, A. O. 98
philosophical analysis of *Paradise Lost* 101–3

Index

Masson, David 103
Milton, John
  Accedence Commenced Grammar 57
  An Apology 64
  Areopagitica 13, 23, 32, 35, 62, 66, 67, 96, 97
  Art of Logic 8, 11, 71, 102
  belief in distributive justice 15, 75
  belief in God as prime cause 8, 11, 87
  belief in learning as means to redress oppression 41–2
  belief in man's fall from grace 7, 10, 11, 14, 24, 46
  belief in reason and choice 8
  belief in virtuous political action 44, 45
  Christian Doctrine 18, 23, 30, 31, 32, 45, 101
  commonwealth, *see* Commonwealth, Milton's
  concept of history, *see* History, Milton's Concept of
  conception of *people* 87
  conception of perception 24
  conception of real liberty 28, 97
  criticism of his historical writings 99–101
  Defense of the English People 55
  defines causation 8–12
  distrust of civil power 76, 82, 93
  Doctrine and Discipline of Divorce 23, 52
  Eikonoklastes 103
  elitism 52, 90
  esteem for Oliver Cromwell 45, 59
  fails to posit constant concept of man's nature 6
  idea of conscience 22, 23, 23–4, 36–7
  lack of toleration 96–7
  literary criticism of work 98–9
  materialist conception of creation 7, 26
  "nature" to 15–17
  on censorship 35
  on Christian liberty 22–3, 87–8
  on civil liberty 23
  on death 27
  on divorce 35, 56
  on domestic liberty 23
  on education, *see* Education, Milton's view of
  on faith and good works 27–8
  on free speech 34, 56, 96
  on free will 24, 25, 35
  on God the Father 30
  on good and evil 13, 14, 18, 25–6
  on Holy Spirit 31
  on knowledge preceding judgement 12, 13
  on liberty in political society 22
  on monarchy 77, 93–4, 97
  on nature of Son of God 29–30, 30–1
  on poetry and politics 63–4
  on predestination 25

Milton, John—*continued*
  on rational soul 26–7
  on redemption through Christ 28
  on religious liberty 23
  on truth of God in Scripture 28, 36, 94
  on will of God 24–5
  Paradise Lost 25, 31, 32, 45, 74, 91, 101
  Paradise Regained 44, 45
  perceives different species of liberty 23
  philosophical analysis of work 101–3
  philosophy compared with Hobbes' 91–5
  position after 1660 103
  primitive Christian theology 31–3
  raison d'être of state 88
  refuses toleration to Roman Catholics 21, 35–6, 95–6, 103
  Samson Agonistes 46, 47, 65
  Second Defense 23, 34
  Seventh Academic Exercise (Prolusion) 40–1
  Tenure of Kings and Magistrates 73, 84, 89, 97, 103
  theological agreement with Origen 32–3
  theological agreement with St. Augustine 33
  theological unorthodoxies 33
  Treatise of Civil Power in Ecclesiastical Causes 76
  view of Christian commonwealth 44, 72, 76
  view of equality and goodness 89–90, 97
  view of man's place in nature 33–5
  view of sin 17, 18, 19, 88
  view of tragedy 46, 47
Monk, George 71, 82
More, Henry
  Account of Virtue 13
  "On the Liberty of Conscience" 96
More, Thomas 61

Nicea, Council of 31

Origen 32–3
Overton, Richard 101

Pelagianism 7
Plato 53, 58, 61, 65, 66
  Laws 54, 56, 58, 60, 61, 62, 64
  on danger of poets 64
  on education 54, 61, 62
  Republic 56
  tripartite division of essences 58, 60
Polybius 78, 80

Ramus 8
Robins, Henry
  If This be Heresy: A Study of Milton and Origen 32
Rump Parliament, 1660 71

St. Augustine of Hippo 7, 33, 73
  City of God 17

idea of original sin   17–18, 18–19
St. Peter
  on obedience to God   22
Salamasius   55
Samuel, Irene   62, 64
Saurat, Denis
  Milton: Man and Thinker   5
  on duality of man   7
  on Milton   5–6
Strauss, Leo
  persecution thesis   103
Sumner, Bishop   31

Thoreau, Henry   104

Tillyard, Phyllis   40
Trinity, the   30

Williams, N. P.
  Ideas of the Fall and of Original Sin, The   18
  theory of "seminal identity"   18
Williams, Roger   96
Winstanley, Gerrard   101
Wolfe, Don   98
  evaluation of Milton   99–101
  Milton in the Puritan Revolution   100